PRESENTED TO:

Dee Emma Neff

FROM:

_____

DATE:

Jan 24, 2002

GOD'S LITTLE
DEVOTIONAL BOOK
FOR LEADERS

GOD'S LITTLE
DEVOTIONAL BOOK
FOR LEADERS

Tulsa, Oklahoma

God's Little Devotional Book for Leaders
ISBN 1-56292-479-6
Copyright © 1997, 2001 by Honor Books, Inc.
P. O. Box 55388
Tulsa, Oklahoma 74155

Manuscript compiled by W. B. Freeman Concepts, Inc.,
Tulsa, Oklahoma

INTRODUCTION

Leadership. Ask ten different people what it means to be a leader and you'll get ten different answers. Leadership is a multi-faceted issue. There are business leaders, church leaders, political leaders, community leaders, family leaders, and so on. However, the principles of good leadership apply whether you're in a position to lead hundreds of people, ten people, or one person. Likewise, the pitfalls of bad leadership can trip you up whether you run a large corporation, a small business, or a growing family.

God's Little Devotional Book for Leaders contains stories of leaders, past and present, to encourage, inspire, and motivate you to be the best leader you can be. The devotions in this book will refresh your soul and remind you what leadership is all about. They point out the character traits necessary to be a leader people want to follow. As you read, meditate on the principles emphasized and be encouraged as you walk the path toward your dreams, bringing others with you as you go.

THE SECRET OF SUCCESS IS TO DO THE
COMMON THINGS UNCOMMONLY WELL.

Mr. Boswell, the owner of a hardware store, was looking for a young man to hire. Several dozen young men responded to his ad, but he eventually narrowed his choice down to three: Ted, John, and Bob. Then he devised a final test. He gave each of them a new screwdriver set with an innovative design and told them to deliver it to Mr. C. M. Henderson at 314 Maple Street.

After awhile, Ted phoned the store to ask whether the number was actually 413, rather than 314. Later, he returned saying there was no house at that address.

When John came back, he reported that 314 Maple was a funeral parlor and that Mr. Henderson had lived at 314-1/2, but had moved away.

8

Bob took longer than the other two young men. Like John, he also discovered that Mr. Henderson had moved away but had managed to secure his new address and had gone there. Mr. Henderson didn't recall ordering the screwdriver, but when Bob pointed out its unique features and told him the price, Mr. Henderson decided he wanted the screwdriver and paid for it on the spot.

Which young man was hired? Bob, of course. He was given a task to do and he did it. A leader doesn't let any obstacle stop him from reaching his goals. Persistence and patience produce payoff.

Do you see a man skilled in his work?
He will serve before kings; he will
not serve before obscure men.
PROVERBS 22:29 NIV

After his parents were brutally murdered in North Vietnam, Ri moved to South Vietnam. While there, Ri went to school and eventually became a building contractor. He prospered greatly until he was arrested while on a trip north. After being imprisoned in North Vietnam for three years, he finally escaped and made his way south, only to be charged as a spy for the north!

When he learned that the U.S. was pulling out of South Vietnam, he gave all his worldly possessions in exchange for passage on a small overcrowded fishing boat. He was later picked up on the high seas by an American ship and taken to the Philippines. Once there, he lived in a refugee camp for two years, until he was allowed to come to the United States.

THE WAY TO GET TO THE TOP IS TO GET OFF YOUR BOTTOM.

Once he arrived in the U.S., Ri's cousin offered both him and his wife jobs in his tailor shop. Even though their net pay was only $300 a week, they were determined to succeed. For two years, they lived in the back room of the tailor shop and took sponge baths so they could save every penny possible.

Within two years, they had saved $30,000 and bought out the cousin's business. It was only then that they rented an apartment.

Today, Ri is a millionaire. Hard work and frugal living can bring a dream into reality! A leader isn't leading if he's not moving forward.

The soul of a lazy man desires,
and has nothing; But the soul of
the diligent shall be made rich.

PROVERBS 13:4 NKJV

11

NEVER, NEVER, NEVER . . .
GIVE UP.

In the 1880's, some of the finest engineers in the world were called in to give their opinions about the possibility of building a railroad through the Andes Mountains. One by one, groups of engineers were presented with various possible routes, and one by one they reported the job couldn't be done. Finally, as a last resort, a Polish engineer named Ernest Malinowski was consulted. Malinowski had a tremendous reputation, but by this time, he was sixty years old.

Malinowski not only assured the representatives of the participating nations that the job could be done, but that he was the man for the job. Thus, at the start of his seventh decade, he began overseeing the building of the highest railroad in the world.

The railroad wound its way through the Andes, through sixty-two tunnels, and across thirty bridges. One tunnel was 4,000 feet long and 15,000 feet above sea level. Revolutions held up construction twice, and once, Malinowski had to flee for his life to Peru. In spite of all the obstacles, the feat was accomplished and is considered one of the great engineering marvels of the world.

Obstacles are *meant* to be hurdled.

Let us not grow weary while doing good, for in due season we shall reap if we do not lose heart.
GALATIANS 6:9 NKJV

Professor Basil L. Gildersleeve of Johns Hopkins University was once interviewed for *The Saturday Evening Post*. At the time, the elderly professor was considered the greatest Greek scholar in the nation, and his work had been honored by numerous organizations and societies around the world.

The interviewer asked Professor Gildersleeve what he considered to be the highest award or compliment he had ever received. He thought for a moment, and then replied, "I believe it was when one of my students said, 'Professor, you have so much fun with your own mind!'"

> TO LOVE WHAT YOU DO AND FEEL THAT IT MATTERS— HOW COULD ANYTHING BE MORE FUN?

Behavioral researchers have discovered that when people enjoy their work and feel it is meaningful, they are more productive, more open to improvement, and are more concerned about the quality of their work. As their levels of productivity and quality rise, they become more efficient and actually begin to earn more money—either through promotions, pay raises, or a broader customer base. As their income increases, they tend to enjoy their work even more!

For a leader to be truly effective, he must find pleasure in his work. Find something you sincerely enjoy doing, then do it well. Success will surely follow!

When you eat the labor of your hands, You shall be happy, and it shall be well with you.

PSALM 128:2 NKJV

THE TEST OF A FIRST-RATE WORK IS THAT YOU FINISH IT.

The Brooklyn Bridge, which links Brooklyn to Manhattan Island, is one of the most famous bridges in the world. At the time it was first conceived in 1883, however, bridge-building experts throughout the world told the designer, a creative engineer by the name of John Roebling, that his idea wouldn't work.

Roebling convinced his son Washington, who was also an engineer, that his idea had merit. The two of them developed the concept, resolved the problems others had forecast, and enthusiastically hired a crew to build their bridge.

After only a few months of building, a tragic on-site accident took John's life and severely injured Washington, who became unable to talk or walk. Everyone thought the project would have to be abandoned, since the

Roeblings were the only ones who knew the dynamics of building the bridge.

Washington, however, could still *think,* and he had a burning desire to see the bridge finished. As he lay in his hospital bed, he had an idea. He would communicate with the engineers by using one finger to tap out in code on his wife's arm what he wanted her to tell them.

Washington tapped out his instructions for thirteen years until the bridge was built!

Leaders are not only self-starters, they are finishers.

I have fought a good fight,
I have finished my *course.*
2 TIMOTHY 4:7

Prizefighter James J. Corbett made many memorable statements during his colorful career, but perhaps his most famous was when he was asked, "What is the most important thing for a man to do to become a champion?" Corbett replied, "Fight one more round."

Nearly all successful people have that perspective. Thomas Gray wrote seventy-five drafts of "Elegy Written in a Country Churchyard" before he was satisfied with his poetic masterpiece.

> DREAMS
> DON'T WORK
> UNLESS
> YOU DO.

S. N. Behrman, an American playwright, wrote plays for eleven years before he sold one. Somerset Maugham earned only $500 in his first ten years as a writer. While working full-time in a factory, Enrico Caruso studied voice for a dozen years before he became a successful performer. George

Gershwin composed almost one hundred melodies before he sold his first one—for $5. During his first five years as a writer, Zane Grey couldn't sell a single story.

Don't be discouraged if your dream doesn't come true immediately. Continue to pursue your craft or talent. Study and learn. Grow by experience. Keep working. The victory goes to those who are willing to fight "one more round!"

The desire of the sluggard puts him
to death, For his hands refuse to work.
PROVERBS 21:25 NASB

CLEAR YOUR MIND
OF <u>CAN'T</u>.

Irwin, a junior naval officer, was discharged from military service after he was diagnosed with cancer—standard military procedure at the time. The loss of his job was quite a blow, but he was determined to get back both his health ***and*** his job. With faith and dogged determination, he battled the disease that tried to take over his body. At one point, he was given only two weeks to live, but eventually, his cancer was brought under control.

Irwin then focused his attention on his desire to become a naval officer. He discovered, however, that regulations forbade reinstatement of a person discharged with cancer. Everyone told Irwin, "Give up. It would take an act of Congress to get reinstated." Their advice gave him an idea—he would pursue an act of Congress!

President Harry S. Truman eventually signed into law a special bill that allowed Irwin W. Rosenberg to reenlist and become a rear admiral in the United States Seventh Fleet!

The thought "Where there's a will . . . there's a way" is applicable to nearly every circumstance in life. When our will lines up with God's will, with His help we will be able to accomplish *anything!*

I can do all things through
Christ who strengthens me.
PHILIPPIANS 4:13 NKJV

Many people face the temptation to slack off once they have achieved a goal. At that point, it's easy to let go of yesterday's insecurities and insufficiencies and accept the illusion that one has arrived.

Professional athletes are especially aware of the danger of such complacency. Even while competing at their peak performance, they face the challenge of preparing themselves for the time when their skills fade and the adulation ends. Those who don't prepare, often settle into marginal careers, and some hit bottom.

> LAZINESS TRAVELS SO SLOWLY THAT POVERTY SOON OVERTAKES HIM.

In the 1960's, Dave Bing was the NBA's leading scorer in his second year as a Detroit Piston. Today, he is still considered one of basketball's greatest players.

Bing thought ahead. Before he went pro, he attended Syracuse University. His advisors suggested he skip the serious courses and earn an "easy" degree. Bing refused, and took tough business classes instead.

During his pro years, he continued his education, reading voraciously on road trips and taking off-season jobs at a bank, a steel mill, and the Chrysler Corporation. Today, he is the CEO of three multimillion-dollar companies that employ more than 300 people and is one of the most successful black businessmen in the nation.

Don't let one success keep you from pressing on to bigger and better things. Constantly set new goals, and you will attain things you never dreamed were possible.

Yet *a little sleep, a little slumber, a little folding of thy hands to sleep: So shall thy poverty come as one that travelleth; and thy want as an armed man.*
PROVERBS 24:33-34

> LIFE IS A COIN. YOU CAN SPEND IT ANY WAY
> YOU WISH, BUT YOU CAN ONLY SPEND IT ONCE.

In ***Miracle on the River Kwai,*** Ernest Gordon tells how Scottish soldiers were forced by their Japanese captors to work on a jungle railroad. They worked in deplorable conditions, under barbarous guards.

One day, a shovel was declared missing. The officer in charge became enraged, demanding that the missing shovel be produced or he would kill ***all*** of the men. The officer pulled his gun. It was obvious he meant what he said.

After several tense moments, a man finally stepped forward. The officer put his gun away, picked up the shovel, and beat the man to death right in front of the other prisoners. They were allowed only to pick up his bloody corpse and carry it with them to a second tool check. There, the tools were recounted and all shovels were accounted for—there had never been a missing shovel. There had simply been a miscount at the first check point.

Word of the incident quickly spread through the entire prison camp. An innocent man had been willing to die to save the others. The incident had a profound effect, binding the prisoners together in deep loyalty. It was that loyalty, in part, that gave the men strength to survive until they were liberated.

Personal sacrifice is inspiring to others. It brings hope and encouragement to weary souls. It produces growth and maturity. There is no true leadership without some kind of sacrifice.

For what is your life? It is even a vapor that appears for a little time and then vanishes away.
JAMES 4:14 NKJV

Noel Borja of Malaybalay, Bukidnon, Philippines would have been the youngest Philippine multimillionaire on record. Alas, it was not to be.

Borja had thirty days in which to appear before his grandfather's executor so that he might receive the $116 million that his grandfather left him, as his sole heir. Unfortunately, the letter from the executor ended up in the dead-mail section of the Bureau of Post, and the deadline expired. Borja never appeared.

> DILIGENCE IS THE MOTHER OF GOOD FORTUNE.

Why didn't Borja receive the notice? He had moved from a boarding house in Manila without leaving a forwarding address. His own negligence left him without a solid basis on which to appeal.

The opposite of diligence is not necessarily laziness, but often, negligence. We should be certain to take care of routine tasks, follow normal procedures, and fill out necessary forms.

Borja lost far more than money because of his lack of diligence. A new standard of living, a new opportunity for giving, and a new outlook on life were all within his grasp.

Diligence will always bring an abundant reward.

The hand of the diligent makes rich.
PROVERBS 10:4 NKJV

Cathy Guisewite is the creator of the very popular syndicated cartoon strip "Cathy." In the comic strip Cathy routinely has encounters with her mother, who is always full of advice for her unmarried, career-oriented daughter. In real life, Cathy's mother has been known to offer her advice from time to time.

Guisewite once said: "I believe very strongly in visualizing goals way beyond what seems humanly possible. I got this from my parents. When my mother first suggested I submit some scribbles to a syndicate, I told her I knew nothing about comic strips. Mom said, 'So what? You'll learn.' When I pointed out that I didn't know how to draw, she said, 'So what? You'll learn.' All parents believe their children can do the impossible. They thought it the minute we were born, and no matter how hard we've tried to prove them wrong, they all think it about us now. And the really annoying thing is, they're probably right."

When we face challenges that lie just beyond our ability, we enter into the realm of faith and hope. It is as we face new frontiers in our lives that we truly encounter what our Creator has endowed us to do. Don't be afraid to desire to accomplish *more* in life.

One thing I do: forgetting what lies behind and reaching forward to what lies ahead.
PHILIPPIANS 3:13 NASB

He had been expelled from college, and his business attempts had failed. Now, as he stood on the windswept shores of Lake Michigan one wintry night, the 32-year-old took one last look at the sky above him as he prepared to cast himself into the freezing water.

It was an overpowering moment. He felt a rush of awe as he saw the starry Heavens, and the thought seared his mind, *You have no right to eliminate yourself. You do not belong to you.* R. Buckminster Fuller walked away from the lake and started over.

UNHAPPINESS IS IN NOT KNOWING WHAT WE WANT AND KILLING OURSELVES TO GET IT.

From that point on, he embarked on a journey that led him into careers as an inventor, engineer, mathematician, architect, poet, and cosmologist. He eventually won dozens of honorary degrees and a Nobel Prize nomination. Fuller wrote two dozen books, circled the globe fifty-seven times, and told millions about his dreams for the future.

The inventor of the geodesic dome, he seldom repeated himself in lectures that sometimes lasted three to four hours on topics that ranged from education to the origin of life.

The day Buckminster Fuller encountered hope was the day he began to find meaning for his life.

There is always a reason to hope. Hope gives us the strength to walk away from failure and move on to success.

What profit hath a man of all his labour which he taketh under the sun?
ECCLESIASTES 1:3

> EFFICIENCY IS DOING THINGS RIGHT.
>
> EFFECTIVENESS IS DOING THE RIGHT THING.

Illinois is considered one of the most prosperous states in the nation today. Many regard an action taken by Stephen Douglas as the origin of that prosperity.

The nation was undergoing a financial depression in the mid-1800's, and state governments began to panic about their potential financial losses. Pennsylvania refused to pay its debts, although it was considered a rich state at the time. Illinois, a poor state at that time, felt justified that it might also take this route in confronting its debt.

When Stephen Douglas heard of this possibility, he opposed the idea with all his might. Although he was seriously ill, he insisted that he be carried on a stretcher to his place in the state legislature. Lying on his back, he made an historic resolution: "That Illinois be honest." His motion touched the deepest sense of morality in every member of the legislature. It was overwhelmingly adopted. The practice of repudiation was dealt a deathblow. The result was that Illinois had to find a new way out of its financial slump—a way that turned out to be one of investment, growth, and eventually, prosperity.

Doing the right thing always pays off, usually not right away, but the momentary relief of an easy solution is nothing compared with the eternal joy of choosing right.

Do what is right and good in the sight of the Lord, so that it may go well with you.
DEUTERONOMY 6:18 NRSV

In *A Closer Walk,* Catherine Marshall writes: "One morning last week He gave me an assignment: *for one day I was to go on a 'fast' from criticism. I was not to criticize anybody about anything.*

"For the first half of the day, I simply felt a void, almost as if I had been wiped out as a person. This was especially true at lunch. . . . I listened to the others and kept silent. . . . In our talkative family no one seemed to notice. Bemused, I noticed that my comments were not missed. The federal government, the judicial system, and the institutional church could apparently get along fine without my penetrating observations. But still I didn't see what this fast on criticism was accomplishing—until mid-afternoon.

A STATUE HAS NEVER BEEN SET UP IN HONOR OF A CRITIC.

"That afternoon, a specific, positive vision for this life was dropped into my mind with God's unmistakable hallmark on it—joy! Ideas began to flow in a way I had not experienced in years. Now it was apparent what the Lord wanted me to see. My critical nature had not corrected a single one of the multitudinous things I found fault with. What it **had** done was to stifle my own creativity."[1]

Let us not therefore judge one another.
ROMANS 14:13

DON'T EQUATE ACTIVITY WITH EFFICIENCY.

The story is told of the manager of a minor league baseball team who became completely disgusted with his center fielder's performance. From where he sat in the dugout, all he saw was a lot of running around and missed catches—activity, but not much productivity. The center fielder always seemed to have "faded" to the wrong side of the field—there, but not having any effect. The manager eventually ordered the player to the dugout and assumed the position himself!

The first ball that came his way took a bad hop and hit the manager right in the mouth. The next hit was a high fly ball to center, which the manager lost in the glare of the sun. It bounced off his forehead. The third ball that came his way was a hard line drive that he charged valiantly, only to have the ball soar just above his outstretched glove.

At that, the manager ran back to the dugout, grabbed the center fielder by his uniform, and shouted, "You've got center field so messed up that even I can't do a thing with it!"

Efficiency isn't a matter of excessive motion. It's a matter of doing only the motion necessary to get the job accomplished.

One of the attributes that makes a leader a leader is knowing which motions to perform.

Let all things be done
decently and in order.
1 CORINTHIANS 14:40

The world always looks brighter when viewed with a smile:

Laugh a little now and then
*   It brightens life a lot;*

You can see the
*   brighter side*
*   Just as well*
*   as not.*

Don't go mournfully
*   around,*
*   Gloomy*
*   and forlorn;*

Try to make your
*   fellow men*
*   Glad that you*
*   were born.*

(Author Unknown)

THE MOST WASTED OF ALL DAYS IS THAT ON WHICH ONE HAS NOT LAUGHED.

It actually takes more muscles to frown than it does to smile. Beyond that, laughter has other very practical therapeutic results. It sends endorphins to the brain, which bring about a sense of well-being and calm. It energizes the body. It releases one's mind from depression and turns it toward goals, dreams, and triumphs. It makes time go by faster and menial chores more enjoyable.

Furthermore, when shared with friends and family, laughter builds relationships. At the end of a busy, tiring day, a happy home is a refuge for each family member, young and old.

Find a reason to enjoy a hearty laugh today!

A happy heart makes the face cheerful, but heartache crushes the spirit.
PROVERBS 15:13 NIV

"Big Red" Blake Wesley, a former NHL hockey player, seemed to have it all—money, luxury, a sweet and pretty wife, and three sons. However, when the injuries of his sport caused him to experience constant pain, Blake turned to painkillers, then alcohol, and eventually drugs. He became increasingly irresponsible as a father and husband, so his wife took their sons back home to Oregon until he faced his life head-on.

Told by his coach that his eight-year career was over until he straightened out his life, Blake found himself alone in a dark, seedy hotel room. Tired and angry, he hit bottom. At that point, he remembered the Lord. Falling to his knees, he yielded his life—including the awful weight of his failures and sins—to the Great Physician, with no strings attached.

Within minutes, his healing had begun. Blake still faced months of counseling and rehabilitation, but an inner work had started that culminated in complete restoration of his family and his life.

Time spent with God today will be the seed that grows into a new tomorrow.

Walk in wisdom ... redeeming the time.
COLOSSIANS 4:5

Shortly after Booker T. Washington became head of the Tuskegee Institute in Alabama, he was walking past the house of a wealthy family. The woman of the house, assuming Washington was one of the yard workers her husband had hired, asked him if he would chop some wood for her. Professor Washington smiled, nodded, took off his coat, and chopped the wood. When he carried the armload of wood into the woman's kitchen, a servant girl recognized him and rushed to her mistress to tell her of his identity.

> A GREAT MAN IS ALWAYS WILLING TO BE LITTLE.

The next morning, the woman appeared in Washington's office. Apologizing profusely, she said repeatedly, "I did not know it was you I put to work."

Washington replied with generosity, "It's entirely all right, madam. I like to work, and I'm delighted to do favors for my friends."

The woman was so taken with his manner and his willingness to forgive that she gave generous gifts to the institute and persuaded many of her wealthy acquaintances to do likewise. In the end, Washington raised as much money for the institute from this one act of chopping wood as he did from any other fund-raising event!

A great leader is never beyond hard work. The willingness to serve others is the essence of true leadership.

"But the greatest among you shall be your servant."
MATTHEW 23:11 NASB

43

AN HONEST MAN'S WORD
IS AS GOOD AS HIS BOND.

The former president of Baylor University, Rufus C. Burleson, once told an audience, "How often I have heard my father paint in glowing words the honesty of his old friend Colonel Ben Sherrod. When he was threatened with bankruptcy and destitution in old age and was staggering under a debt of $850,000, a contemptible lawyer told him, 'Colonel Sherrod, you are hopelessly ruined, but if you will furnish me $5,000 as a witness fee, I can pick a technical flaw in the whole thing and get you out of it.'

"The grand old Alabamian said, 'Your proposition is insulting. I signed the notes in good faith, and the last dollar shall be paid if charity digs my grave and buys my shroud.' He carried me and my brother Richard once especially to see that incorruptible old man, and his face and words are imprinted upon my heart and brain."

People will remember us for our *kept* promises and our honesty, especially when we could have profited from not telling the truth. The character of your word is your greatest asset, and honesty is your best virtue.

Let your "Yes" be "Yes," and your "No," "No."
JAMES 5:12 NKJV

Can one person really make a difference in the world today?

One New Yorker thought so. He was determined to be complimentary to every person he saw, every day. A friend asked him, "Do you even compliment cab drivers?" The man said, "Certainly! If I am nice to one cab driver, he's likely to be nice to his next twenty fares, at a minimum. If they are in turn nicer to the shopkeepers, waitresses, and their own families, that one gesture of goodwill might influence at least a thousand people!

> AN UNUSED
> LIFE IS
> AN EARLY
> DEATH.

"Now, if only three people that I talk to today have a happier day because of what I say to them, I might indirectly influence the attitude of 3,000 people. If a few of those I talk to are teachers, or people who have contact with more than the usual number of people . . . why my good mood might touch more than 10,000 lives. Not one other thing I do today is likely to have that kind of impact!"

Pass on a portion of what you have today. If you have nothing but your own smile, goodwill, and joy—pass it on! You *can* make a difference.

The fool folds his hands and
consumes his own flesh.
ECCLESIASTES 4:5 NASB

IN THE LONG RUN MEN HIT ONLY WHAT THEY AIM AT.

From an early age, Larry lived and breathed the sport of golf. As a teenager, he was ranked one of the top sixteen young golfers in the nation. Then, at the beginning of his senior year of high school, Larry was in an automobile accident. He suffered severe injuries, but the most devastating was that his left arm had to be amputated just below the elbow.

Larry had never heard of a one-armed golfer, but then again, he didn't know that it couldn't be done! As Larry began to swing a few golf clubs at the rehab center, his mother and a psychologist sought out someone who could design a prosthetic hand for him. After several months of practice with his new hand, Larry hit a ball one day. When it landed more than 200 yards away, he knew he was "back." He rejoined his high-school team, scoring even better than before, and is now in college on a golf scholarship!

"Don't think of your missing limb as something that makes you a lesser person," Larry once told an audience of children who had lost limbs. "Think of it as something that can make you stronger. I would love to be the first pro golfer with a prosthetic hand. But I also know that if I don't succeed, I won't be a failure. We only fail if we don't try."

Therefore I do not run uncertainly (without definite aim).
1 CORINTHIANS 9:26 AMP

A young man once placed this ad in a New York City newspaper:

Inexperience is the most valuable thing a man can bring to a new job. A man of inexperience, you see, is forced to rely upon imagination and verve, instead of timeworn routine and formula. If you're in the kind of business which is penalized by routine and formula thinking, then I'd like to work for you. Inexperience is my forte. I'm twenty-five years old and have the ability to become enthusiastic and emotionally involved in my work.

> ENTHUSIASM IS CONTAGIOUS. IT'S DIFFICULT TO REMAIN NEUTRAL OR INDIFFERENT IN THE PRESENCE OF A POSITIVE THINKER.

He was immediately hired by a chain of photo studios.

Be enthusiastic today about every area of your life—your family, your friends, your coworkers, your work, your hobbies, your church, but especially your dreams and your potential to achieve them. Enthusiasm fuels hope and joy. People gravitate toward a person who radiates hope and joy, bringing with them unique opportunities, sound advice, and valuable resources.

Finally, brethren, whatever is true ...
honorable ... right ... pure ... lovely ...
of good repute, if there is any excellence
and if anything worthy of praise,
let your mind dwell on these things.

PHILIPPIANS 4:8 NASB

A designer in Dallas, Texas, was once asked by a client to build a large, elaborate model. It was one that called for several building interiors and hundreds of human figures. The model was to be created in a scale of one inch to five feet, which meant that each of the human figures was only a little more than an inch in height. Each one had to be hand-painted, using a brush with a single hair.

As the designer hunched over his table one day, painstakingly painting the figures and then carefully gluing them in place, one of his employees asked him, "Don't you find this tedious?"

The designer replied, "Tedious? My goodness, no! I've loved making and painting models ever since I made my first model airplane at age seven. I just can't believe someone is actually paying me to do this!"

Whether you work with your hands or your mind, loving what you do is the secret to having "fun" while you make money. Indeed, work will cease to be "work."

A kindergarten teacher once said about her class of five-year-olds, "They build and tear down and rebuild more in a day than most construction workers do in weeks, but they never call it work. They call it play!"

Stand at the crossroads and look;
ask for the ancient paths, ask where
the good way is, and walk in it, and
you will find rest for your souls.
JEREMIAH 6:16 NIV

Juan grew up in Puerto Rico, the son of a sugar-cane plantation foreman. He lived with his family of eight in a three-room shack with a dirt floor and no toilet. His first job, at the age of six, was to drive oxen to plow the cane fields eight hours a day for $1, with no breaks. Juan looks back on those days as tedious but important in his life.

EXPERIENCE IS NOT WHAT HAPPENS TO A MAN. IT'S WHAT A MAN DOES WITH WHAT HAPPENS TO HIM.

It was in the cane fields that he learned to be on time, work hard, and be loyal and respectful to his employers. His job and small income were a great source of self-esteem. At age seven, he got a job at a golf course spotting balls for golfers.

Juan began to dream of playing golf and earning enough money to buy a bicycle. The more he dreamed, the more he thought, *Why not?* He made a club out of a guava limb and a piece of pipe, and then he hammered an empty tin can into a ball. Next, he dug two small holes in the ground and hit the ball back and forth between them. He practiced "golf" with the same intensity he had put into his job in the cane field, only this time he was driving golf balls with a club, rather than oxen with a stick. He got good—*very* good.

In his thirty-one years as a pro golfer, Juan "Chi Chi" Rodriguez won twenty-four tournaments and earned $4 million.

No matter how or where you started out in life, you can use your circumstances for your benefit. Difficult circumstances can make you more determined to succeed, if you keep the right attitude.

For whatever is born of God overcomes the world; and this is the victory that has overcome the world—our faith.

1 JOHN 5:4 NASB

> THE PERSON WHO KNOWS "HOW" WILL
> ALWAYS HAVE A JOB. THE PERSON WHO
> KNOWS "WHY" WILL ALWAYS BE HIS BOSS.

After Thomas Edison's fame had become international, he was advised to have scientists come to his lab and help him understand just why some of his inventions had worked. Edison didn't see much use for it, but being open-minded, he consented to the idea. As a result, a brilliant research scientist from Germany came to his lab to explain to him the principles behind some of his innovations.

Edison handed the man a globe that had been twisted into a gourd-like shape and said, "Give me the cubic content of this."

Weeks passed, and eventually Edison sought out the man to ask him why he hadn't replied. The scientist began to give him a lengthy explanation about the difficulties of solving such a problem with higher mathematics. Edison then picked up the globe, took it over to a nearby sink, and filled it with water. He poured the water into a measuring tube, and holding up the tube he said, "This is the cubic content."

The solutions to most problems are probably far more simple than we *think* they might be. They usually stem from an understanding of basic principles, the *whys* of life.

How much better to get wisdom
than gold! And to get understanding
is to be chosen rather than silver.
PROVERBS 16:16 NKJV

According to designer Judyth van Amringe, author of *Home Art: Creating Romance and Magic With Everyday Objects,* "You don't need a lot of money—just a little imagination—to do what I do." Judyth often finds the materials she works with at flea markets. In one instance, she took an old frame, covered it with macaroni shells, hiding the frame's cracks and chips, and painted it in "seaside" colors. In another case, she covered the legs of a warped pine table—a junk shop find— with plastic ivy and fruit to give it an exotic look.

> DEVELOP THE HUNTER'S ATTITUDE . . . WHEREVER YOU GO, THERE ARE IDEAS WAITING TO BE DISCOVERED.

Where does she get her ideas? "I have no idea," she says, "but I've always wanted to put my personal touch on things. . . . Don't be afraid to experiment. The point is to customize things to your own style, your own way of living, and in the process, make life more amusing."[2]

Judyth began her business by designing scarves, jewelry, and gloves, and then went on to decorate homes. Today, she is able to devote herself full-time to her design work in New York City.

Look around today. How do you *wish* the world to look? It is out of your own vision that you can begin to brighten your world.

"For everyone who keeps on asking receives; and he who keeps on seeking finds; and to him who keeps on knocking, [the door] will be opened."
MATTHEW 7:8 AMP

★ ★

TAKE FIRST THINGS FIRST. THAT PROCESS
OFTEN REDUCES THE MOST COMPLEX HUMAN
PROBLEMS INTO MANAGEABLE PROPORTIONS.

★ ★

Charlie Brown comes up to bat. He is determined, as always, to do well. Someday, just
maybe, his team will win a game. And someday,
just maybe, he might be a baseball hero.

Strike THREE! Charlie Brown has struck out
once again. He returns to the sidelines and
slumps down on the bench. "Rats! I'll never be
a big-league player. I just don't have it! All my
life I've dreamed of playing in the big leagues,
but I know I'll never make it."

Lucy turns to console him in her inimitable
way. "Charlie Brown, you're thinking too far
ahead. What you need to do is set more
immediate goals for yourself."

Charlie looks up, appearing to brighten at
the prospect of something positive that might
come from all the negatives he has been
experiencing. "Immediate goals?"

"Yes," Lucy advises, "start with the next inning. When you go out to pitch, see if you can walk out to the mound without falling down!"

Too often, we allow ourselves to stumble over our daily chores because our minds are in the clouds, dreaming about the person we will become someday. It's okay to dream about tomorrow, but *live* in the present.

"But seek ye first the kingdom of God, and his righteousness; and all these things shall be added unto you."
MATTHEW 6:33

A teenager named Buck was walking to his father's apartment from a subway stop one day when he suddenly realized that two men were flanking him.

"Give me your wallet," one of the men insisted. "I have a gun. Give me your wallet or I'll shoot."

"No," Buck said.

"Hey, man, you don't understand. We're robbing you. Give me your wallet."

"No."

"Give me your wallet or I'll knife you."

"No."

"Give me your wallet or we'll beat you up."

By now the robber was *pleading* more than he was demanding.

"No," Buck said once again. He kept walking and, a few steps later, realized that the two

> COURAGE IS
> RESISTANCE TO
> FEAR, MASTERY
> OF FEAR. NOT
> THE ABSENCE
> OF FEAR.

men had disappeared. As he related this story to a friend, the friend asked, "Weren't you scared?"

Buck replied, "Of course I was scared!"

"Then why didn't you give them your wallet?"

"Because," Buck answered matter-of-factly, "my learner's permit is in it."

While it may be wise to give in to the demands of a thief, the first and best answer to fear is always "No!"

Therefore, take up the full armor of God, that you may be able to resist in the evil day, and having done everything, to stand firm. Stand firm therefore.
Ephesians 6:13-14 nasb

THE BUSINESS OF FINDING FAULT IS VERY EASY,
AND THAT OF DOING BETTER IS DIFFICULT.

Lloyd John Ogilvie wrote in *Let God Love You,* "The hardest time to be gentle is when we know we are right and someone else is obviously dead wrong. . . . But the greatest temptation for most of us is when someone has failed us and has admitted it, and their destiny or happiness is in our hands. We hold the power to give or refuse a blessing.

"Recently, a dear friend hurt me in both word and action. Each time we met . . . I almost began to enjoy the leverage of being the offended one. His first overtures of restitution were resisted because of the gravity of the judgment I had made. He had taken a key idea I had shared with him in confidence and had developed it as his own before I had a chance to use it. The plagiarism of ideas had been coupled with the use of some of my written material, reproduced under his name. . . . The most difficult thing was to surrender my indignation and work through my hurt. . . .

"Finally, the Lord got me where He wanted me. . . . His word to me was clear and undeniable, 'Lloyd, why is it so important to you who gets the credit, just so My work gets done?' I gave up my right to be what only God could be as this man's judge and savior. The gentle attitude began to flow."[3]

When we withhold forgiveness, it not only hurts the person we don't want to forgive, it hurts us. Our creativity and joy in life are stifled. When we forgive, we release peace and restoration to the forgiven, and to ourselves.

Therefore you are without excuse, every man of you who passes judgment, for in that you judge another, you condemn yourself; for you who judge practice the same things.
ROMANS 2:1 NASB

Are you aware of the difference between a boss and a leader? Consider these ten traits:

1. A boss creates fear in a staff. A leader builds confidence.

2. A boss says, "I." A leader says, "We."

3. A boss *knows* how a job should be done. A leader *shows* how a career should be forged.

4. A boss relies on authority. A leader relies on cooperation.

5. A boss drives. A leader leads.

> REMEMBER THE DIFFERENCE BETWEEN A BOSS AND A LEADER: A BOSS SAYS "GO!"— A LEADER SAYS "LET'S GO!"

6. A boss fixes blame. A leader solves problems and fixes mistakes.

7. A boss rules over the *problem* 10 percent of the work force. A leader

works alongside the *cooperative* 90 percent.

8. A boss eventually causes resentment to grow. A leader fosters growing enthusiasm.

9. A boss makes work drudgery. A leader makes work interesting.

10. A boss sees problems as disasters that will destroy the company. A leader sees problems as opportunities that a united staff can overcome and turn into growth.

Are you just a boss, or are you a leader?

Let us go up at once, and possess it;
for we are well able to overcome it.
NUMBERS 13:30

After the fall of France in World War II, a fable began to circulate about the fate of England. The story was told that in July 1940, Hitler and Mussolini invited Churchill to Paris for a secret conference. They met at a tea table beside a famous carp pool. The Führer opened the dialog: "England is finished, Churchill! Sign this document admitting defeat, and all Europe will have peace tomorrow!" Churchill said quietly, "I don't agree that we have lost the war."

Hitler pounded the table and cried, "Ridiculous!"

"Why not settle this with a wager?" Churchill asked.

Hitler responded, "What's the bet?"

Churchill said, "See these big carp in the pool? Let's wager that the first to catch one without using customary fishing equipment will be the winner."

Hitler and Mussolini agreed and the Fuhrer quickly pulled out a revolver and emptied it at the nearest fish. The water deflected the bullets. Next, Mussolini jumped into the pool and tried to catch a carp with his bare hands. He failed.

"Your turn, Churchill," said Hitler.

Churchill began to repeatedly dip his spoon into the pool and toss the water over his shoulder. "What are you doing?" cried Hitler. Churchill replied, "It will take a long time, *but we are going to win the war!*"

Seest thou a man diligent in his business?
he shall stand before kings.
PROVERBS 22:29

When Everett Alvarez, Jr. was given only thirty seconds to prepare a five-minute speech for his Toastmasters' Club, he quickly thought back through his life. He recalled a time when he searched through his neighbor's trash for empty soda pop bottles to turn in at the corner grocery for a penny each.

All day, he carried bottles to the store in his red wagon, until he had a small mountain of coins— just enough to buy a card and a candy bar. They were surprise birthday presents for his mother. When he returned home, his mother demanded, "Where have you been? I've been searching everywhere for you!"

As his mother continued her questioning, Ev blubbered through his tears, "I was collecting bottles to get you these." He handed her the

> HE WHO HAS A <u>WHY</u> TO LIVE CAN BEAR ALMOST ANY <u>HOW</u>.

unsigned card and the candy bar that had nearly snapped in two in his pocket. His mother then began to cry as she proudly placed the gifts on a window ledge so all the neighbors might see.

Ev's speech spoke to the hearts of his audience—a group of fellow prisoners of war at the infamous Hanoi Hilton prison camp in North Vietnam. For many of the men, it was the heritage of sacrificial family love that was their "suit of armor," the "why" that enabled them to survive years of nightmarish torture.

Never forget your promises to me
your servant, for they are my only hope.
They give me strength in all my troubles;
how they refresh and revive me!
PSALM 119:49-50 TLB

GLDB

NOTHING IS PARTICULARLY HARD IF YOU DIVIDE IT INTO SMALL JOBS.

John Erskine, a well-known author and professor, once wrote that he learned the most valuable lesson of his life when he was only fourteen years old. It came from his piano teacher.

"How many times a week do you practice, and how long do you practice each time?" the teacher asked.

John replied that he usually tried to practice once a day, generally for an hour or more. The teacher warned, "Don't do that. When you grow up, time won't come in long stretches. Practice in minutes, whenever you can find them—five or ten before school, after lunch, between chores. Spread your practice throughout the day, and music will become a part of your life."

Looking back, John saw that advice as a good formula against "burnout." He also saw it as a way to live a complete life as a creative writer, apart from his regular teaching duties. He wrote the bulk of his most famous work, **Helen of Troy,** while commuting between his home and the university.

To make a day count, make each minute count!

He [Abram] divided his forces against them by night, he and his servants, and defeated them, and pursued them.
GENESIS 14:15 NASB

F. B. Meyer, a minister in England, once told of the following experience to a few of his friends: "It was easy to pray for the success of G. Campbell Morgan when he was in America. But when he came back to England and took a church near to mine, it was something different. The old Adam in me was inclined to jealousy, but I got my heel upon his head, and whether I felt right toward my friend, I determined to act right.

"My church gave a reception for him, and I acknowledged that if it was not necessary for me to preach Sunday evenings I would dearly love to go and hear him myself. Well, that made me feel right toward him. But just see how the dear Lord helped me out of my difficulty. There was Charles Spurgeon preaching wonderfully on the other side of me.

> IT IS THE CHARACTER OF VERY FEW MEN TO HONOR WITHOUT ENVY A FRIEND WHO HAS PROSPERED.

He and Mr. Morgan were so popular, and drew such crowds, that our church caught the overflow, and we had all we could accommodate."

When we give up being jealous of a friend, we often find in its place a deeper friendship and a greater blessing.

A friend loves at all times.
Proverbs 17:17 nrsv

GLDB

> A MAN WHO DOES NOT READ GOOD
> BOOKS HAS NO ADVANTAGE OVER
> THE MAN WHO <u>CAN'T</u> READ THEM.

After experiencing numerous failures in business and politics, Abraham Lincoln still maintained his daily habit of reading. A critic scoffed, "What good is all that education? It has never earned you a decent living."

Lincoln replied, "Education is not given for the purpose of earning a living; it's learning what to do with a living after you earn it that counts."

One of America's greatest reading advocates is Jim Trelease. He has devoted nearly two decades to promoting what he considers the most important social factor in our lives today. "The more you read," he says, "the smarter you grow. The smarter you grow, the longer you stay in school. The longer you stay in school, the more money you earn. The more you earn, the better your children will do in school. So if you hook a child with reading,

76

you influence not only his future but also that of the next generation."

Reading researchers agree. They have long seen a correlation between the time a person spends reading and the number of innovative ideas and creative solutions a person has. Reading affects a person's ability to reason, and his ability to communicate, by providing an extended and accurate vocabulary.

Spend some time reading today. It will be time well spent, investing in your personal growth, which affects your future success. As the poster often seen hanging in libraries and classrooms says, "Succeed . . . Read!"

Apply thine heart unto instruction, and thine ears to the words of knowledge.
PROVERBS 23:12

Two women who once lived in a convalescent center had each suffered an incapacitating stroke. Maggie's stroke had caused paralysis on her left side. Rachel's stroke had caused permanent damage to her right side. Both women were devastated by what had happened to them, since they assumed they would never be able to pursue a pastime they had genuinely enjoyed throughout life—playing the piano.

> LIFE CAN'T GIVE ME JOY AND PEACE; IT'S UP TO ME TO WILL IT. LIFE JUST GIVES ME TIME AND SPACE; IT'S UP TO ME TO FILL IT.

Then, one day, Maggie and Rachel met and began talking about their lives. When they realized they both had an interest in music, an idea emerged. When approached with the idea, the convalescent center's director brought them a piano and helped each woman sit on an elongated bench in front of it. Maggie played the right-hand notes, while

Rachel played the left-hand! Not only did they make beautiful music together, but they formed a long and endearing friendship.

God's design for us is that we work *together,* live *together,* and have fun *together.* When we choose to share our time and space with others, we will reap the rewards of joy and peace.

I have set before you life and death, the blessings and the curses; therefore choose life, that you and your descendants may live.
DEUTERONOMY 30:19 AMP

GLDB

NEVER ALLOW YOUR SENSE OF SELF TO
BECOME ASSOCIATED WITH YOUR SENSE OF JOB.
IF YOUR JOB VANISHES, YOUR SELF DOESN'T.

Writing in *Brown Book Magazine* in 1904, Bessie Anderson Stanley gave this eloquent definition of success:

He has achieved success who has lived well, laughed often and loved much; who has enjoyed the trust of pure women, the respect of intelligent men and the love of little children; who has filled his niche and accomplished his task; who has left the world better than he found it, whether by an improved poppy, a perfect poem, or a rescued soul; who has never lacked appreciation of earth's beauty or failed to express it; who has always looked for the best in others and given them the best he had; whose life was an inspiration; whose memory a benediction.

Our true sense of identity—which gives our life meaning and a genuine sense of success—

is not bound up in tasks, deadlines, or projects. It lies in relationships—the day-to-day associations we have at home, in our community, and in church—as well as our relationship with our Heavenly Father. It is as we relate to *people*—family, friends, colleagues—that we develop a true sense of who we are.

What advantage does man have in all his work Which he does under the sun? A generation goes and a generation comes, But the earth remains forever.
ECCLESIASTES 1:3,4 NASB

Edith Schaeffer writes in *What Is a Family?:*
"We knew a family in Lausanne some twenty years ago, a mother with a son and daughter who sometimes lived with her at the then-temporary apartment and went to a day school—or sometimes went to boarding school. Father was an importer-exporter who traveled most of the time around and around the world. When the teenage girl asked, 'Why, Dad, can't you ever be home? Why can't you do less and have some time together with us?' The reply was, 'I have to earn enough . . .

> MEN FOR THE SAKE OF GETTING A LIVING FORGET TO LIVE.

so that if I die you'll have enough.' . . . That family lived in a 'temporary' situation for years. . . . ***When*** did that man picture a family life being 'normal'—when was the temporary portion going to end?

"We all know examples of homes where both father and mother work 'until we get another car' or 'until we pay for this house' or 'until we buy a summer cottage' . . . months go by, years go by . . . never will these in my imaginary family know what it is like to have Mother open the front door or the kitchen door and say, 'Hi! How was your day? Smell the bread baking? I'm making orange rolls. . . . Come on in and have a glass of milk.' *Never.*"[4]

The best you can give your child, is you.

Every man should eat and drink,
and enjoy the good of all his labour,
it is the gift of God.
ECCLESIASTES 3:13

> ★★★★★★★★★★★★★★★★★★ ✦ ★★★★★★★★★★★★★★★★★★
>
> THE ART OF BEING WISE IS THE ART
> OF KNOWING WHAT TO OVERLOOK.
>
> ★★★★★★★★★★★★★★★★★★★★★★★★★★★★★★★★★★★★

The Mysterious Island, a novel by Jules Verne, is the story of five men who escape a Civil War prison camp by hijacking a hot-air balloon. Very quickly, they realize the wind is carrying them out over the ocean. As the hours pass, they see the horizon receding and realize that they are also losing altitude. Since they have no way of heating the air in the balloon, they begin to throw some of the excess weight overboard. Shoes, coats, and weapons are reluctantly discarded, yet they rejoice that the balloon begins to rise.

Soon, they draw dangerously close to the waves again and begin to toss their food overboard. Better to be aloft and hungry! Yet a third time, the balloon begins to descend and this time one of the men suggests they tie together the ropes that connect the balloon to the basket in which they are riding, and then sit on the ropes and cut away the heavy basket. The very floor they had been standing on falls away, and the balloon rises once again.

Suddenly, they spot land. With not a minute to spare, they jump into the water and swim to an island. Their lives are spared, not because of any great heroics, but because they had learned what they could live without. They learned what they could overlook and survive without.

A man's wisdom gives him patience;
it is to his glory to overlook an offense.
PROVERBS 19:11 NIV

As a young boy, Fritz wanted nothing more than to play the violin. He listened with rapt attention to violin music. His parents encouraged his interest by paying for him to have lessons. Fritz didn't make as much progress as they had hoped he would however, and after a few years he eventually quit the lessons.

> WE IMPROVE OURSELVES BY VICTORIES OVER OUR SELF. THERE MUST BE CONTESTS, AND WE MUST WIN.

Over the next several years, through college and young adulthood, Fritz studied medicine, but he failed to complete medical school. He joined the army, and failed to be promoted. He tried and quit many other pursuits. Realizing that the little bit of success he had enjoyed in life had been related to the violin, he went back to his violin instructor and said, "I want to play."

She said, "Fine, I'll take you back as a student, but only if you acquire the irreplaceable quality that is necessary for you to become a great violinist. You must exhibit undefeatable determination."

This time, Fritz Kreisler persevered in his pursuit of music—the first time he had truly persevered in anything he had attempted—and eventually Carnegie Hall was filled with his music.

Now every athlete who goes into training conducts himself temperately and *restricts himself in all things. They do it to win a wreath that will soon wither, but we [do it to receive a crown of eternal blessedness] that cannot wither.*

1 CORINTHIANS 9:25 AMP

HE THAT HAS LEARNED TO OBEY WILL KNOW HOW TO COMMAND.

One of the things that virtually every employee wishes he or she had with superiors is better communication. Unfortunately, once those same employees rise to top-level management, they too forget to communicate with those they manage.

That isn't the case with Sally Frame Kasaks, who became CEO of Ann Taylor in 1993. She placed a new emphasis on quality with "more and better communication with employees at all levels." In 1994, sales rose 31.3 percent!

Paul Kahn had a similar agenda when he became chairman and CEO of SafeCard Services in 1993. He and his head of operations, Richard Interdonato, changed the internal company strategy to emphasize:

- Open doors.

- Visibility—Interdonato spends about 40

percent of his time "just talking with people."

- Sharing information through a daily newsletter and frequent open forums with employees.

The company had record revenues in 1994, with earnings up 13.1 percent from the year before.[5]

As you rise in authority, always remember what issues were important to you as an entry-level employee!

And the Lord shall make thee the head, and not the tail; and thou shalt be above only, and thou shalt not be beneath; if that thou hearken unto the commandments of the Lord thy God, which I command thee this day, to observe and to do them.

DEUTERONOMY 28:13

On opening day of the 1954 baseball season, the Cincinnati Reds hosted the Milwaukee Braves. Two rookies began their major league careers in that game. The Reds won 9-8. Without dispute, the star of the game was Jim Greengrass, the rookie who hit four doubles in his first major-league outing. Sports commentators almost immediately began hailing him as the next superstar. Plus, he had a made-for-baseball name!

> TRIUMPH IS JUST "UMPH" ADDED TO TRY.

The other rookie that day had a dismal start. He was 0-5, but he kept swinging, kept trying, and kept playing. His powerful batting performances over the years eventually earned Henry "Hank" Aaron a place in Baseball's Hall of Fame!

Another sports example of adding "umph" to try is Walter Payton. During a Monday night football game between the New York Giants and the Chicago Bears, one of the announcers noted that Payton, the Bears' running back, had just passed nine miles in career rushing yardage. The other announcer added ruefully, "Yeah, and that's with someone knocking him down every 4.6 yards!"

Being knocked down isn't the same as being knocked out, unless you stay down. Give it some "umph" and keep trying!

And let us not be weary in well doing: for in due season we shall reap, if we faint not.

GALATIANS 6:9

THERE IS NO FAILURE EXCEPT IN NO LONGER TRYING.

In 1902, an aspiring young writer received a rejection letter from the poetry editor of *The Atlantic Monthly*. Enclosed with a sheaf of poems the 28-year-old poet had sent was this curt note: "Our magazine has no room for your vigorous verse." He rejected the rejection, however, and went on to see his work published. His name was Robert Frost.

In 1905, the University of Bern turned down a Ph.D. dissertation as being fanciful and irrelevant. The young physics student who wrote the dissertation rejected their rejection and went on to develop some of his fanciful ideas into widely accepted theories. His name was Albert Einstein.

In 1894, a sixteen-year-old found this note from his rhetoric teacher at Harrow, in England, attached to his report card: "A conspicuous lack of success." The young man rejected the rejection and went on to become one of the most famous speakers of the twentieth century. His name was Winston Churchill.

Reject the rejection you may receive today, and go on to achieve real achievement!

Let us hold fast the confession of our hope without wavering, for He who promised is faithful.

HEBREWS 10:23 NKJV

Don was hungry for success. At the age of thirty, he owned his own business, drove a sports car, had a house at the beach, a condo close to the office, and was part owner of a boat. He was tall and good-looking, every bit the eligible bachelor, and he seemed determined to date as many women as possible.

At the age of thirty-one, Don was stricken with cancer. Everything in his life abruptly changed. To his credit, he was able to make a major leap in his life from living for himself and according to his own will, to expressing a need for God and a desire to live according to God's will.

> HE HAS ACHIEVED SUCCESS WHO HAS LIVED WELL, LAUGHED OFTEN, AND LOVED MUCH.

Don reevaluated his priorities and four years later said: "I've been in several hospitals and had a number of different treatments. I've been in remission twice, and twice the disease has returned. I've seen people die, and I've seen people live. And above all, I've learned what's important and what's not."

During the course of his illness, Don married one of the women he had been dating and a year later, his wife gave birth to a daughter. Don says of his life today, "I wouldn't trade what I've been through. Having things is not living. Loving and knowing God—that's living. The fact is, whether I'm here on earth or in Heaven, loving and knowing God is all that matters."

Go then, *eat your bread in happiness, and drink your wine with a cheerful heart; for God has already approved your works.*

ECCLESIASTES 9:7 NASB

When Jim was diagnosed with cancer, his company heartlessly dumped him. In battling the disease, he used up all of his insurance fund, and his life savings. A church deacon went to visit Jim and asked boldly, "Have you prepared for your life after death?"

Jim became irate, and swearing at the man he said, "All you Christians think about is what's going to happen after I die. If your God is so great, why doesn't He do something about the real problems of life?" He bitterly complained that he was leaving his wife penniless and his daughter without money for college. Then he ordered the man to leave his house.

The man thought about what Jim had said and soon returned. "I offended you and I'm sorry," he said. "I've been working on your problems. A realtor I know has agreed to sell your house and give your wife his commission.

Some of us will make your house payments until the house is sold. The earnings from your house should pay for your daughter's college. Also, the owner of an apartment building up the street has offered to give your wife a unit, with free utilities, plus a monthly salary in exchange for managing the complex."

Jim cried like a baby. He could finally *hear* the Gospel message with an open heart.

And though I have the gift of prophecy, and understand all mysteries, and all knowledge; and though I have all faith, so that I could remove mountains, and have not charity, I am nothing.

1 CORINTHIANS 13:2

Most baseball fans know that from 1960 to 1966, the record for the most stolen bases was held by Maury Wills of the Los Angeles Dodgers. In 1962, Wills seemed to set fire to the path between first and second, stealing 104 bases in one season.

Maury Wills set another record during those same years—a rather dubious one. In 1965, a year in which he held the top honors for the most stolen bases, he also held the record for being thrown out the most times while attempting to steal a base! He was caught trying to steal thirty-one times that year.

YOU CANNOT STEAL SECOND BASE WHILE KEEPING ONE FOOT ON FIRST BASE.

We don't really remember the bases Wills *didn't* steal, only the ones he did. But the fact is, had Maury Wills allowed himself to become discouraged at being thrown out, he never would have set the records he did. He was a man determined to "go for it," to do his best, to take the risk of trying, to push the envelope a little in the lead he took off first base, to get a jump on the pitch and fly to second base in a race against the catcher. Once Wills set out to steal a base, there was *no turning back*.

Whatever it is you desire to do today, do it with your whole heart and all your determination—no looking back.

A double minded man is
unstable in all his ways.
JAMES 1:8

> ★★★★★★★★★★★★★★★★ ✦ ★★★★★★★★★★★★★★★★
>
> THE SIZE OF YOUR SUCCESS IS DETERMINED
>
> BY THE SIZE OF YOUR BELIEF.
>
> ★★★★★★★★★★★★★★★★★★★★★★★★★★★★★★★★★★

In 1931, Ted and Dorothy Hustead decided to move to a town that had four things: a good school, a Catholic Church, a doctor, and an opportunity. They wanted to open their own pharmacy. They eventually chose Wall, South Dakota, as the perfect location. To others, however, Wall seemed to be in the middle of nowhere—somewhere between the Black Hills and the Badlands.

The first year was a tough one—thick dust, intense heat, and strong winds. In their desire to move on to a more welcoming place, tired, throat-parched travelers rarely stopped. Then, Ted and Dorothy came up with an idea. They made a sign that read: FREE ICE WATER AT WALL DRUGSTORE. The sign became something of a novelty. They made more signs and put them farther and farther from Wall—

eventually, as far as Europe, India, Korea, Egypt, and the North Pole!

All druggists, of course, made "free" ice water available for their customers. But nobody else had thought to advertise the luxury. Eventually, some 4,000 to 6,000 customers a day stopped at Wall Drugstore.

When you take a step toward your dream, you open yourself to creative ideas and solutions. Taking that big step gives you hope and optimism, which are essential elements for creativity. Dream big, step big, and do big things.

"Everything is possible for him who believes."

MARK 9:23 NIV

When Daniel Webster was just beginning his career as a lawyer, he took a case for a fee of $20. The case turned out to be a very difficult one, and in preparing for it, Webster had to make a trip to Boston, which in itself cost more than Webster was going to earn as a fee. He was determined, however, to do a thorough job on the case and win it, which he did. In retrospect, it seemed like a small case, but at the time, it was a big victory.

> BE GREAT IN THE LITTLE THINGS.

Years later, a large company approached Webster on short notice, asking him to undertake a case for which they were willing to pay a very handsome fee—in fact, a fee quite stunning at the time. As Webster reviewed the case, he found that it was almost identical to the one he had researched and won nearly twenty years before for the fee of only $20. He took the case, and just as before, the verdict was in favor of his client.

A familiar phrase holds great truth: "Nothing is lost in God's economy." He uses *all* our efforts that are motivated by goodwill and a generous and faithful heart. Sometimes the reward is immediate. Sometimes it can take a lifetime, but the reward will most definitely come.

> *"He who is faithful in a very little thing is faithful also in much; and he who is unrighteous in a very little thing is unrighteous also in much."*
> LUKE 16:10 NASB

OPPORTUNITIES ARE
SELDOM LABELED.

In 1864, during a crisis at the Telegu Mission in India, a civil engineer named, John E. Clough offered to go to the mission to help. The missionary board of the American Baptist Missionary Union had some misgivings about why a civil engineer who had never gone to seminary would want to go to India, but they admired his zeal, so they authorized his trip.

Over time, it became apparent why God had called him to India. During the great famine of 1876-77, Clough supervised the digging of the Buckingham Canal. His position enabled him to hire thousands of starving natives and thus, secure them wages and a means of buying food.

Because of this practical but lifesaving act, the Telegus were open to receiving what Clough truly desired to give them: copies of the

Scriptures and the life-changing message of Jesus Christ.

Only God can truly see the beginning and the ending of any situation or circumstance. He alone knows the very best person for each job in His Kingdom.

God is always in the process of preparing you for your next step. From where you are, it may not look like the most logical way to go, but once you take the step, it will become apparent why you're there.

As we have therefore opportunity, let us do good unto all men, *especially unto them who are of the household of faith.*

GALATIANS 6:10

A film editor once said, "I had this date the other night with a woman who wanted to walk along the beach. I'm wearing a twelve-hundred dollar suit, a seventy-five dollar tie, a hundred-and-fifty-dollar shirt, and two-hundred-dollar shoes. It costs me fifteen dollars to clean my suit and six dollars to have my shirt hand washed.

"I don't even want to think about what it would cost if I should get a drop of spaghetti sauce on my tie. And this woman wants me to roll up my pants and walk along the beach! All I can think about is how much it's going to cost me if she wants to sit down on the sand. Here's the bottom line that I have to ask myself: Can I afford to wear my own clothes?"

Another man, a lawyer, once said, "I don't think I'm trapped on this treadmill forever, but

> MANY A MAN HAS FOUND THE ACQUISITION OF WEALTH ONLY A CHANGE, NOT AN END, OF MISERIES.

I'm certainly involved with it right now. . . . It's the old merry-go-round of how much money is enough money? And it's never enough. Three years ago I thought, "Just a little more. . . . " Now I make twice as much, and it's still not enough."[6]

Money should be a means toward living a generous, giving life—not an end in itself. When having money becomes their only goal, people not only hoard it, but they close themselves off to genuine living.

He who loves money will not be satisfied with money, nor he who loves abundance with its *income. This too is vanity.*

ECCLESIASTES 5:10 NASB

> I AM DEFEATED, AND KNOW IT, IF I MEET
> ANY HUMAN BEING FROM WHOM I FIND
> MYSELF UNABLE TO LEARN ANYTHING.

For a number of years, Jamie Buckingham periodically worked with healing evangelist Kathryn Kuhlman. He wrote in *Coping with Criticism:* "Although Miss Kuhlman was very sensitive to criticism, she never let it deter her from her goal. Instead, she used it to help her get there. . . .

"Shortly after she went on nationwide television with her weekly program, she received a letter from a public school official. . . . 'I love you and love your program,' he wrote. 'It would have been much better, however, if you didn't have to spend so much time tugging at your skirt trying to pull it down over your knees. It was really distracting. Why don't you wear a long dress instead?' Kathryn read the letter. 'You know, he's right,' she said to her secretary. She never wore another street-length dress on her TV program.

"A lesser person would have responded with anger, or passed it off as just another senseless remark. But she was not that sort of lesser person. She heard. She coped. She let it help her toward her goal of communicating. All of which was possible because there was no root of bitterness to give a bad taste to everything that came into her life which presented another viewpoint."[7]

A wise man will hear, and will increase learning; and a man of understanding shall attain unto wise counsels.

PROVERBS 1:5

On a cold Saturday morning in January, in a small Wisconsin town on the southern shore of Lake Superior, an annual dog sled derby was about to begin. The course had been staked out by little fir trees secured to the ice.

The racers were all children—from large boys with several dogs and big sleds to one little boy who had only a small sled and one small dog. On the signal, the sleds took off and the little fellow was soon so far behind he hardly seemed to be in the race. Then, about halfway through the course, the second-place team tried to move into first place. The sleds came too close and the dogs began to fight. As each subsequent sled came upon the fight, more dogs became involved. The scene was soon one big, seething knot of kids, sleds, and dogs.

> SUCCESS SEEMS TO BE LARGELY A MATTER OF HANGING ON AFTER OTHERS HAVE LET GO.

All thought of *racing* had vanished from the minds of the sledders. However, the one little fellow and his dog managed to skirt the others and went on to win the race!

Part of any success is refusing to become distracted. Pursue your goals today, without wavering or hesitating. Keep your eyes on the finish line.

Let us hold fast the confession of our hope without wavering, for He who promised is faithful.
HEBREWS 10:23 NKJV

GLDB

> IF YOU KEEP SAYING THAT THINGS
> ARE GOING TO BE BAD, YOU HAVE
> A CHANCE OF BEING A PROPHET.

Cheryl continually complained that she didn't make enough money, couldn't afford the things she wanted, and therefore, wasn't ever going to amount to anything. A counselor said to her, "You're throwing your energy away complaining instead of using it to get ahead."

"But you don't understand. The job is the problem, not me," Cheryl countered.

The counselor said, "Your low-paying job may be a problem and your boss may demand too much, but if you are continually that upset, you are causing *yourself* more harm than either the job or the boss."

"What can I do?" she asked.

The counselor said, "You can't control your boss or the job, but you can control how you *feel* about them. Change your attitude."

Cheryl took her advice. When she stopped whining about her life, people around her noticed. She got a promotion, and with her new job status, she was more marketable. Within several months, she was transferred out of the department into a position with even higher pay and a more supportive boss.

Awful is a state of *attitude*. A change in attitude will change the state of things!

Thou art snared with the words of thy mouth, thou art taken with the words of thy mouth.

PROVERBS 6:2

On their way home from a lifetime of service as missionaries in Africa, an elderly couple found themselves on the same ocean liner as President Teddy Roosevelt, who was returning from a big game hunting expedition.

The couple watched in awe at the fanfare given the President and his entourage. When the ship docked in New York, a band was waiting to greet him, the mayor was there to welcome him, and the newspapers heralded his return.

A GREAT DEAL OF GOOD CAN BE DONE IN THE WORLD IF ONE IS NOT TOO CAREFUL WHO GETS THE CREDIT.

Meanwhile, the missionary couple slipped quietly off the ship and found a cheap apartment. They had no pension, they were in poor health, and they were discouraged and fearful. The husband, especially, could not seem to get over how the President had received such acclaim, while their decades of service had gone without notice or reward. "God isn't treating us fairly," he complained bitterly to his wife.

"Why don't you pray about it?" his wife advised.

A short time later, the wife noticed a change in her husband's demeanor. "What happened?" she asked. The man replied, "The Lord put His hand on my shoulder and simply said, *'But you're not home yet!'*"

So then, whether you eat or drink,
or whatever you may do, do all
for the honor and *glory of God.*
1 CORINTHIANS 10:31 AMP

> SHOW ME A MAN WHO CANNOT BOTHER TO
> DO LITTLE THINGS AND I'LL SHOW YOU A MAN
> WHO CANNOT BE TRUSTED TO DO BIG THINGS.

Not many years ago, a young man was working very hard as a section hand for a railroad company. His superiors offered him the opportunity to work in the shipping office for a few days, and he jumped at the chance.

During that time, the superintendent asked the young substitute clerk for some vital facts and figures. "Have them on my desk when I get back in three days," he said. The young man didn't know anything about bookkeeping, but he worked three days and three nights without sleep. He had the facts and figures ready when the superintendent returned.

The young man, of course, won the admiration of his superintendent, and as soon as a permanent position opened, he recommended the young man for the job. Over time, the young man was promoted many times, and each time, he was applauded for his thoroughness and trustworthiness. He eventually became vice-president of the Ralston Purina Company in St. Louis, Missouri.

Give each difficult task and each mundane chore or request your best effort. You will be rewarded not only according to the tasks you complete, but for the *way* in which you complete them!

"You have been faithful and *trustworthy over a little; I will put you in charge of much."*
MATTHEW 25:21 AMP

A small-town chamber of commerce once invited a man to address their annual banquet. The speaker was asked to be motivational, since the town's economy had been bad that year and people were discouraged.

During his presentation, the speaker took a large piece of white paper and made a black dot in the center of it with a marking pen. He then held the paper up before the audience and asked, "What do you see?" One person replied, "I see a black dot." The speaker said, "Fine. What else do you see?"

> FAITH IS DARING THE SOUL TO GO BEYOND WHAT THE EYES CAN SEE.

Others chimed in, "A black dot." The speaker asked, "Don't you see anything besides the dot?" The audience responded with a resounding "No!"

"But you've overlooked the most important thing," the speaker replied. "You've missed seeing the sheet of paper!" He then went on to explain, "In our lives, we are often distracted by small, dot-like failures. They keep us from seeing the blessings, successes, and joys that are far more important than the disappointments that try to monopolize our energy and attention. I encourage you to focus on the big picture of what is right rather than the small view of what is wrong."

Are you so preoccupied today with what is, that you've lost sight of what *can* be? Step back and see the bigger picture!

Now faith is the substance of things hoped for, the evidence of things not seen.
HEBREWS 11:1 NKJV

GOOD WORDS ARE WORTH MUCH AND COST LITTLE.

One day, a young altar boy was serving the priest at a Sunday Mass being held in the country church of his small village. The boy, nervous in his new role at the altar, accidentally dropped the cruet of wine. The village priest immediately struck the boy sharply on the cheek and in a very gruff voice, shouted so that many people could hear, "Leave the altar and don't come back!" That boy became Tito, the Communist leader who ruled Yugoslavia for many decades.

One day in a large city cathedral, a young boy was serving a bishop at a Sunday Mass. He, too, accidentally dropped the cruet of wine. The bishop turned to him, but rather than responding in anger, gently whispered with a warm twinkle in his eyes, "Someday you will be a priest." That boy grew up to become Archbishop Fulton Sheen.

Words have power. The childhood phrase, "Sticks and stones can break my bones, but words can never hurt me," simply isn't true. Words can hurt. They wound—sometimes deeply.

But words can also reward, build self-esteem, create friendships, give hope, and render a blessing. Words can heal and drive accomplishment.

Watch what you say today! Your words can produce life or death.

Pleasant words are a honeycomb, Sweet to the soul and healing to the bones.
PROVERBS 16:24 NASB

It's impossible to please everybody all of the time. Any person who lives in the public eye knows that the public is fickle! A person can be immensely popular one day, and go virtually unnoticed the next.

A better way to live is described in this poem:

There's only one method of meetin' life's test:

Jes' keep on a-strivin' an' hope for the best;

Don't give up the ship an' quit in dismay;

'Cause hammers are thrown when you'd like a bouquet.

This world would be tiresome we'd all get the blues,

If all the folks in it jest held the same views;

I DON'T KNOW THE SECRET TO SUCCESS BUT THE KEY TO FAILURE IS TO TRY TO PLEASE EVERYONE.

So finish your work, show the best of your skill,

Some folks won't like it, but other folks will.

(Author Unknown)

A pop song of two decades ago seemed to echo this sentiment in saying, "You can't please everybody, you've got to please yourself." However, a Christian is called to an even higher standard: "Don't try to please anybody other than the Lord. Follow in His footsteps, keep His commandments, and do your best to fulfill His will for your life." Ultimately, pleasing Him is all that matters.

"No one can serve two masters; for either he will hate the one and love the other, or he will hold to one and despise the other."

MATTHEW 6:24 NASB

GLDB

IT IS A MISTAKE TO LOOK TOO FAR AHEAD.
ONLY ONE LINK OF THE CHAIN OF DESTINY
CAN BE HANDLED AT A TIME.

Sometimes we can become so preoccupied with the future that we lose all sense of the present! We can become so concerned about our next shot, our next match, our next game, our next project that we have no concentration or mental power left for the present moment. We become crippled in the now when we constantly live in anticipation of what's next.

Leon Lett learned that the hard way. A defensive tackle for the Dallas Cowboys, Lett hadn't scored a touchdown since he was in grade school. But in the 1993 Super Bowl, he got his chance. The Buffalo Bills' quarterback fumbled right in front of him and Lett was there to scoop up the ball and head for the goal line.

Seeing no one between him and a sure touchdown, Lett threw out his arms when he reached the ten-yard line, thrilled at his uncontested sixty-four-yard scramble to the

124

end zone. Unfortunately, he didn't hear Don Beebe, the Bills' wide receiver, in pursuit of him. At the one-yard line, Beebe lunged forward and knocked the ball from Lett's outstretched hand, stealing the touchdown from him.

Stay focused on the task at hand. Keep yourself in the here and now. Then you'll be better prepared for tomorrow when it comes.

"Therefore do not be anxious for tomorrow; for tomorrow will care for itself. Each day has enough trouble of its own."
MATTHEW 6:34 NASB

Years ago, a corps of civil engineers went to take a look at a dam in Pennsylvania that controlled the waters of several streams that flowed down toward a valley. Concerned by what they saw, they went to the town just below the dam and reported to its officials, "The dam is unsafe. The people of your town are in danger." The officials said, "You're just trying to scare us. The dam is all right. We've heard this before."

That fall, the engineers revisited the dam and came back again, saying, "We are warning you. You are in danger every hour." Again, the people laughed as if to say, "Scare us if you can." In the spring, the engineers again went to the dam, and again they warned the townspeople. Their warning was dismissed.

> IT'S THE JOB THAT'S NEVER STARTED THAT TAKES THE LONGEST TO FINISH.

Fifteen days later, a boy on a horse rode through the valley at a dead run shouting, "Run for your lives! The dam has broken and the water is coming." The people only laughed at him, certain he was only trying to scare them. But in a few minutes, a wall of dirty water struck the town, and in less than thirty minutes, Johnstown was in ruins. More than 3,700 people died.

If you are warned you have a problem, admit that it exists, then don't delay in fixing it. Take action to bring about a solution.

> *The way of the sluggard is blocked*
> *with thorns, but the path of*
> *the upright is a highway.*
> PROVERBS 15:19 NIV

A shopkeeper once fell behind in his payments to one of his vendors. To further complicate matters, he completely ignored three increasingly sharp letters demanding payment. Finally, the vendor appeared in person with a sheaf of unpaid bills under his arm. Holding them out before the shopkeeper, he demanded full payment immediately.

To the vendor's surprise, the shopkeeper didn't hesitate or ask for more time. He simply sat down and wrote out a check, paying him in full. "Is this going to cash?" The vendor asked, suspicious.

"Oh, yes," said the shopkeeper.

"Then why didn't you just send me a check several weeks ago and save us both this unpleasant visit?" cried the vendor.

"Well, at first I didn't have the cash," the store owner admitted, "but I copied your letters and mailed them out to people who owed me. Everybody paid up. Your letters worked so well, I just kept stalling on payment to you in hopes that I might eventually have a full set of your letters for use in my own business!"

Pushing people may result in payment, but not in building good relationships. Be diligent in your own work, never at the expense of another.

He who has a slack hand becomes poor,
But the hand of the diligent makes rich.

PROVERBS 10:4 NKJV

A crude little lifesaving station once stood on a dangerous seacoast known for shipwrecks. The station was only a hut with one small boat, but volunteers tirelessly kept their watch over the churning seas.

Some of those they rescued and others who admired their work began to volunteer. New boats were purchased. New crews were trained. Some of the members raised funds to build a bigger station with newer equipment and better lifesaving systems.

> THE WORLD IS FULL OF WILLING PEOPLE: SOME WILLING TO WORK, THE REST WILLING TO LET THEM.

Over time, the station began to be less of a lifesaving station and more of a boat club, with only a few members actually involved in patrolling the seas and rescuing those in danger. Eventually, so few members of the station were interested in the life-saving missions, they hired professional lifeboat crews to do it, but only when storms arose.

About that time a large ship experienced an explosion in its engine room and began to take on water. Its S O S signal went unnoticed in the lifesaving station—the regular members were too busy with other matters. The ship was already sinking by the time a lifeboat was launched. Many people died.

Would *you* hear an S O S call today, or are you just a member of a yacht club?

Then He said to His disciples, "The harvest is plentiful, but the workers are few."
MATTHEW 9:37 NASB

GLDB

> THE MOST DIFFICULT SECRET FOR A MAN
> TO KEEP IS THE OPINION HE HAS OF HIMSELF.

Most of us come to the lofty opinion we have of ourselves by means of comparison. In our judgment of others, we conclude, "I'm not like *that* person. I'm superior to *those* people." Pride does not exist in a vacuum. In the process of raising ourselves up "on a pedestal," we inevitably leave others in the dust.

A poem by an unknown author addresses this sorry attribute of mankind in a clever way:

> *I dreamed death came the other night;*
> *And heaven's gates swung wide.*
>
> *With kindly grace an angel*
> *Ushered me inside.*
>
> *And there, to my astonishment,*
> *Stood folks I'd known on earth.*
>
> *Some I'd judged and labeled*
> *Unfit or of little worth.*

Indignant words rose to my lips,
* But never were set free;*

For every face showed stunned surprise . . .
* No one expected me!*

Rather than measuring yourself against other people, measure yourself against your own potential. You can always reach farther and dream bigger.

I warn everyone among you ...
[not to have an exaggerated opinion
of his own importance], but to rate
his ability with sober judgment.
ROMANS 12:3 AMP

According to legend, the Apostle John had a tame partridge that he enjoyed feeding and tending. A serious hunter passed by one day and was astonished to see the great apostle playing with a pet bird. He said, "I am surprised, sir, to see you engaged in such an amusement when there are such great matters related to the Gospel with which you could be busy."

The apostle asked in return, "Do you always keep your bow bent?" The hunter replied, "Why, no. That would render it useless. I loosen the string unless I am hunting." The apostle nodded and said, "So I unbend my mind for the same reason."

> NO ONE EVER SAID ON THEIR DEATHBED: I WISH I WOULD HAVE SPENT MORE TIME AT WORK!

One summer, a pastor announced that he wasn't going to take a vacation, since the devil never goes on vacation. A parishioner went home and reread the Gospels to see if Jesus had the same attitude. He found that in His three years of active ministry, Jesus had ten periods of retirement away from the crowds, in addition to nightly rest and Sabbath-day rest! He asked his pastor the next Sunday, "Are you following the devil's example or the Lord's?"

Take time to rest and play with your family. Recreation is just that, *re*creation—a time to renew your energy, as well as your most valuable relationships.

Then I considered all that my hands had done and the toil I had spent in doing it, and again, all was vanity and a chasing after wind.

ECCLESIASTES 2:11 NRSV

No one is useless in this world who lightens the burden of it to anyone else.

Thomas Samson was a Welsh miner. Each day, he put in long, hard hours at the mine—his life in constant danger—just to earn a meager wage. One day, the foreman of the mine came to him and said, "Thomas, I've found an easier job for you above ground. You'll have less to do and earn more money. Are you interested?"

"Oh, yes," said Thomas, "I'm very interested, sir. But, would you consider giving the job to my friend Tregony instead? He isn't as strong as I am, and he's not able to work as hard as I can. I fear the work below in the mine will shorten his life and I will lose my friend. Might he have this job?"

The foreman was moved by Thomas' generosity and gave the job to Tregony. Thomas continued to work hard, and when another above-ground position opened, the foreman again approached Thomas about the job. This time, he accepted the offer. Thomas and Tregony went on to work side-by-side for two decades.

When you selflessly give for another person, you build an honorable reputation. Promotion will surely follow.

*Bear ye one another's burdens,
and so fulfil the law of Christ.*
GALATIANS 6:2

A boy was once so ugly and clothed so shabbily that he was continually tormented by his schoolmates. He turned to reading in order to escape their taunts. At eighteen, he took a job as a bricklayer. He decided, however, that he did not want to be a bricklayer, but a playwright. He forged a new path in his life and was eventually honored by Queen Elizabeth I and decorated by King James. He was Ben Johnson, one of the most brilliant playwrights in England's history.

> DO NOT FOLLOW WHERE THE PATH MAY LEAD—GO INSTEAD WHERE THERE IS NO PATH AND LEAVE A TRAIL.

Oliver Goldsmith was the son of a poor preacher. He was considered to be a sensitive but morbid child. His schoolmaster labeled him, "a stupid blockhead." He earned a college degree, but graduated at the very bottom of his class. He was rejected from becoming a preacher. He tried law, and again was rejected. He borrowed a suit of clothes to take an examination to be an assistant in a hospital, then failed at that as well.

He lived in poverty, was often ill, and once, even pawned his clothes for food. The one thing he wanted to do more than anything was to write. And so he forged a new trail. In the end, he rose above his past to rank among the greatest writers of all time.

Sometimes a way will open up for you. At other times, you may have to open it up!

Your ears shall hear a word behind you, saying, "This is the way, walk in it."
ISAIAH 30:21 NKJV

George Jones began his career as a clerk in a crockery store. He soon gained a reputation as being a bright, ambitious employee—a young man known for good work habits, fine manners, and an easy-going personality. The foremost traits people referred to when praising George, however, were his honesty and trustworthiness. It was this reputation that came to the attention of Henry J. Raymond, a renowned journalist, and together Raymond and Jones started the *New York Times*.

Mr. Jones continued to live up to his reputation. His loyalty to Raymond and his honesty as a businessman won him great repute in New York City.

Then the *Times* began a crusade against Boss Tweed and his corrupt dynasty. Jones received an under-the-table offer of $500,000— a vast sum at the time—from associates of

Tweed. All he had to do was retire to Europe. "You can live like a prince the rest of your days," the man making the offer said. But Jones replied, "Yes, and know myself every day to be a rascal."

A clean conscience can't be bought. That is what makes it so highly valued! Keeping a clean conscience is as simple as deciding to. Decide not to let tempting offers influence you. When you do, God is right there to give you the strength to overcome any temptation.

If our hearts do not condemn us, we have confidence before God.

1 JOHN 3:21 NIV

When Jeremy arrived in the home of Mike and Jo Ann as a foster child, he couldn't dress or feed himself and he wasn't potty-trained. He had been seriously neglected. In his new family, he received good food and a sense of safety and was sent to nursery school and speech therapy. Over one summer, Jeremy grew two inches and gained two pounds. His vocabulary also grew and he was no longer afraid of the dark. Then, three months after he had arrived in Mike and Jo Ann's home, the State sent him to live with his grandparents.

> My OBLIGATION IS TO DO THE RIGHT THING. THE REST IS IN GOD'S HANDS.

As Jeremy was driven away, Jo Ann remembered back to when the family was struggling to cope with Jeremy's problems. She had asked Mike, "Why are we doing this?" The answer came several months later as she and

Mike attended church together. The pastor read from the Scriptures: "He then took a little child whom he set among them and embraced, and he said to them, 'Anyone who welcomes a little child such as this in my name, welcomes me.'" Mike nudged Jo Ann and whispered, *"That's* why we do this."[8]

The Lord never called any of us to be successful—only to be faithful. Our success lies in His hands, and our reward comes from His supply.

If you know that he is righteous,
you may be sure that every one
who does right is born of him.
1 JOHN 2:29 RSV

WHEN YOU SOAR LIKE AN EAGLE, YOU ATTRACT HUNTERS.

When people are unreasonable, illogical, self-centered and arrogant, love them anyway.

When people insist that your goodness contains selfish ulterior motives, do good anyway.

If you are successful, you will win both friends and enemies. People may become jealous of you. Succeed anyway.

If you are honest and frank, you will be both honorable and vulnerable. Some will seek to twist your words against you. Be honest and frank anyway.

If you do good today, some may forget about it by tomorrow. Do good anyway.

If you show yourself to be a big person with great ideas, don't be surprised if you are opposed by small people with closed minds. Think big anyway.

What you have spent years building, some may seek to destroy overnight. Build anyway.

Mark Twain once said, "Always do right. This will gratify most people, and astonish the rest!"

Be of sober spirit, *be on the alert. Your adversary, the devil, prowls about like a roaring lion, seeking someone to devour.*

1 PETER 5:8 NASB

President Theodore Roosevelt once said, "It is not the critic who counts, not the person who points out where the doer of deeds could have done better. The credit belongs to the person who is actually in the arena; whose face is marred by dust and sweat and blood; who strives valiantly; who errs and comes up short again and again; who knows the great enthusiasm, the devotion, and spends himself or herself in a worthy cause; who at best knows in the end the triumph of high achievement; and at the worst, at least fails while daring greatly; so that his or her place shall never be with those cold and timid souls who know neither victory nor defeat."

> THOSE THAT HAVE DONE NOTHING IN LIFE ARE NOT QUALIFIED TO BE JUDGE OF THOSE THAT HAVE DONE LITTLE.

It actually takes very little effort to voice criticism. Judging others requires no degree, no expertise, no background, no qualifications. It requires no investment of time, resources, or self. In other words, it costs nothing. And because of that, criticism is usually worth just that: nothing.

On the other hand, a life well lived is one that has few apologies to make. It is highly invested with self, energy, resources, and time. It is rich in friends, associates, and good deeds. It is built by effort and morality. And because of that, it is beyond value.

"Do not judge, or you too will be judge. For in the same way you judge others, you will be judged."

MATTHEW 7:1-2 NIV

In the introduction to Catherine Marshall's *A Closer Walk,* her husband of twenty-three years, Leonard LeSourd, writes about their marriage in 1959: "Catherine had huge adjustments to make. She sold her Washington dream house to move to Chappaqua, forty miles north of New York City, so that I could continue to commute to my job at *Guideposts* in the city. My children—Linda, ten; Chester, six; Jeffry, three—had been through a deeply unsettling two years, adjusting to a variety of housekeepers. They had mixed feelings toward moving into a new house, and especially toward 'the new Mommie that Daddy's bringing home.'

"Catherine's son, Peter John, nineteen, was going through a period of rebellion at Yale. . . .

"Catherine and I had so many things to pray about that we began to rise an hour early each morning to read the Bible and seek answers together. Her current journal lay open beside us in these pre-dawn prayer times, recording *our* changing needs, *His* unchanging faithfulness."[9]

The more you have crammed into your schedule, and the more problems you have, the more you have to pray about!

Evening and morning and at noon I will pray, and cry aloud, And He shall hear my voice.

PSALM 55:17 NKJV

Was God telling him to stay in London rather than go to China? Thomas Barnardo had come to London for missionary training, only to have a ten-year-old child show him a rooftop where eleven homeless boys were sleeping. Barnardo's heart was touched. He set about finding temporary lodging for the boys.

Other midnight tours of the area revealed many more homeless youth— as many as seventy-three in one night. China would have to wait. God had given him London. Barnardo sold some 30,000 copies of the Scriptures in the public houses and marketplaces to raise money for his work among the children. He was often rejected for defending them, even sustaining physical injury.

EXPECT GREAT THINGS FROM GOD. ATTEMPT GREAT THINGS FOR GOD.

In one attack, he suffered two broken ribs. When a cholera epidemic hit London in 1866, he and others worked tirelessly, only to see thousands die. He eventually opened a "Home for Destitute Boys" and, later, a "Village for Girls." Through the next several decades, he built numerous homes and villages that cared for some 60,000 abandoned children.

Barnardo's missionary desire was put to work by his being "The Father of Nobody's Children." And happily, he lived long enough to see seventeen of the youth he rescued take the Gospel to foreign lands!

"Truly, truly, I say to you, he who believes in Me, the works that I do shall he do also; and greater works than these shall he do; because I go to the Father."

JOHN 14:12 NASB

AH, BUT A MAN'S REACH
SHOULD EXCEED HIS GRASP.

Napoleon saw Italy, but not the Alps. He had an objective, and he knew where he was going. The Alps were simply something to be crossed enroute.

Washington saw the Hessians massed at Trenton. He didn't see the Delaware choked with ice. A frozen river was simply a challenge to be overcome on the way to a victory.

A young man intent on bettering his life and earning a college degree will hold a strong image of "graduation day" in his mind. The exams, long nights of study, and jobs that must be done to pay for tuition and room and board are simply the price that is paid in exchange for a great reward.

A mother about to give birth has her mind and heart wrapped around the baby she will soon hold in her arms. The agony of childbirth is simply something that must be endured to experience the joy of new life.

The majority of people will always see the obstacles that loom in their path. But the truly successful will see the objectives—the goals, the reason, the hope that lies beyond the obstacles.

Those who work through problems reside in the land of success. Those who don't, are lost in oblivion.

But this one thing I do: forgetting what lies behind and straining forward to what lies ahead, I press on toward the goal.

PHILIPPIANS 3:13-14 NRSV

Jane awoke dripping with perspiration, her fever had just broken. Her body was aching, and she was completely drained. She could not imagine speaking that night, and yet, what was she to do? She was the only speaker scheduled for the annual vacation-church-school adult class. To cancel would not only have created somewhat of a crisis, but she felt it would also reflect a failure of her own professed faith that God heals and helps. Instead of canceling, she prayed.

> ANYBODY CAN DO THEIR BEST. GOD HELPS US TO DO BETTER THAN OUR BEST.

Throughout the day, Jane felt no better. Still, mustering all the energy she had, she dressed and drove herself to the meeting. Every five minutes, she found herself thinking, *I cannot do this. Only by God's help will I even make it to the lectern.* Every step, every action, required major effort. She could tell her fever had returned.

Once behind the lectern, however, she found that she had energy to speak a sentence, and then another, and yet another. She spoke with great vitality and clarity of thought for nearly an hour. Upon return home, however, she collapsed into her bed where she stayed and slept for 18 hours.

Jane later said, "What I could not possibly have done in my own strength . . . I did in His strength."

Now glory be to God who by his mighty power at work within us is able to do far more than we would ever dare to ask or even dream of.

EPHESIANS 3:20 TLB

155

SHALLOW MEN BELIEVE IN LUCK . . .
STRONG MEN BELIEVE IN CAUSE AND EFFECT.

The story is told of a farmer who told a friend that he had decided he no longer needed to work. "God will do it for me," the man said.

"Oh, really?" the friend said. "What makes you think that?"

"Well," the farmer said, "do you remember that old shed I used to have? I've been meaning to tear it down for years but lightning struck it last month and burned it to the ground and then the wind came up and blew away all the ashes."

"And on the basis of that, you're going to let God do all your work?" the friend asked.

"Oh, no," the farmer continued. "Last weekend my wife asked me to wash our car, but a big rainstorm blew in before I got to it, and the rain washed the car clean."

156

The friend shook his head in dismay, and before he could say anything further, the farmer asked, "Do you know what I'm doing out here on my porch right now?"

The friend said, "No, what?"

The farmer replied, "I'm waiting for an earthquake to shake my crop of potatoes out of the ground!"

Don't expect God to do what He has empowered and enabled you to do.

Be not deceived; God is not mocked:
for whatsoever a man soweth,
that shall he also reap.
GALATIANS 6:7

Said yesterday to tomorrow:

*When I was young like you,
I, too, was fond of boasting*

*Of all I meant to do.
But while I fell a-
dreaming*

*Along the pleasant
way,
Before I scarcely
knew it,*

*I found I was
to-day!
And as to-day,
so quickly*

*My little course
was run,
I had not time
to finish*

*One-half the things begun.
Would I could try it over,*

*But I can ne'er go back;
A yesterday forever,*

> DOST THOU
> LOVE LIFE?
> THEN DO NOT
> SQUANDER TIME,
> FOR THAT IS
> THE STUFF LIFE
> IS MADE OF.

I now must be, alack!
  And so, my good to-morrow,

If you would make a name
  That history shall cherish

Upon its roll of fame,
  Be all prepared and ready

Your noblest part to play
  In those new fleeting hours

When you shall be to-day.

—The Pacific

Remember how short my time is.
PSALM 89:47

****

DON'T LET YOUR LEARNING
LEAD TO KNOWLEDGE; LET YOUR
LEARNING LEAD TO ACTION.

****

Pat loved children and was quick to volunteer when the call went out for a Sunday school teacher for the five-year-olds. There, she met Andy. He was a likable boy, but he lacked confidence and he rarely smiled.

One Sunday while the class was coloring a Bible scene, Andy became so frustrated he tore his paper in two, threw it on the floor, and crawled under the craft table. Pat thought, *I go where he goes!* And she immediately crawled under the table, where she found Andy muttering, "You're so dumb. You can't even color in the lines." He seemed surprised to see Pat join him under the table.

Pat quickly said, "Who said you always have to stay in the lines? Some of the smartest, most creative kids I've ever known didn't color inside the lines."

Andy stared at her. This was obviously a new idea to him. Then Pat said, "I like your picture. Can I tape it back together and keep it?" Andy was stunned but finally said, "I guess." While Andy watched, Pat taped the pieces together and carefully put the picture in her satchel. As he returned to the craft table, Pat overheard him say, "I *like* coloring!"

Little acts of kindness can mean a lot—especially to "little people."

Be ye doers of the word, and not hearers
only, deceiving your own selves.

JAMES 1:22

In *Traveling Hopefully,* Stan Mooneyham writes:

"I will go, when —
"I will give, after —
"I will obey, but first —

"One can always find reasons for delay, and sometimes they may even seem to be valid reasons. A close friend of mine and I were called to preach about the same time, and we went to university together. I was out mutilating homiletics in rural Oklahoma churches during those four years of study, but my friend insisted he wouldn't preach his first sermon until he had received his Ph.D. That was over thirty years ago. I am still mutilating homiletics, but my friend isn't preaching at all. He never did. Preparation is important, but *doing* is an important part of preparation. . . .

PROCRASTINATION IS THE THIEF OF TIME.

In the Old Testament we hear much about offerings of 'firstfruits.' God's portion came right off the top. Nowadays we are more likely to be known by and for our 'lastfruits.'

"Near the hold button on the hotline to heaven, these classic words would be appropriate:

'If not I, who?

'If not here, where?

'If not now, when?'"[11]

He also that is slothful in his work is brother to him that is a great waster.

PROVERBS 18:9

FORGET YOUR OPPONENTS; ALWAYS PLAY AGAINST PAR.

Bobby Jones, one of golf's greatest players, was only five years old when he first swung a golf club. By the age of twelve, he was winning club tournaments. At the time, he was known for his hot temper, and he soon had the nickname "Club Thrower."

Jones became friends with a man named Grandpa Bart, who worked part-time in the club pro shop. Bart had been an excellent golfer but had retired when arthritis gripped his hands. After Bobby lost the National Amateur Tournament at the age of fourteen, Bart told him, "Bobby, you are good enough to win that tournament, but you'll never win until you can control that temper of yours. You miss a shot—you get upset—and then you lose."

Bobby knew Grandpa Bart was right, and he set to work to improve, not his swing, but his mood swings. When Bobby won a major tournament at age twenty-one, Grandpa Bart said, "Bobby was fourteen when he mastered the game of golf, but he was twenty-one when he mastered himself."

Norms and records are always established in relationship to other people's performance, but the true "standards of success" are established within and then lived out in relationships.

For we wrestle not against flesh and blood.
EPHESIANS 6:12

Back-to-back victories by the Dallas Cowboys at the Super Bowl in 1993 and 1994 may mask the fact that Jimmy Johnson, the team's legendary former coach, knew as much about losing as he did about winning. In 1989, his first season in Dallas, Johnson's team had only one win, and fifteen losses! This overwhelming losing season was only a little worse and a little less humiliating than his first year as a high-school defensive coach, when his team finished the season 0-10.

> NEVER PLAY NOT TO LOSE; ALWAYS PLAY TO WIN.

Johnson said about that first season in Dallas, "We had the worst team in the NFL, but I wouldn't accept anything but being in the Super Bowl."

Johnson kept a positive attitude. If a running back had the ball, he shouted, "Protect the ball," rather than "Don't fumble." To his field-goal kickers he'd say, "Make this," not "Don't miss." After a loss, he'd spend his post-game time plotting the next win, rather than second-guessing what had gone wrong.

The Cowboys responded, and improved. It took four seasons, but Super Bowl rings were on their fingers.[12]

You may not win every contest you pursue, but the person who plays to *win* always has a much better chance!

> *But thanks be to God, Who gives us the victory [making us conquerors] through our Lord Jesus Christ.*
> 1 CORINTHIANS 15:57 AMP

SADDLE YOUR DREAMS BEFORE YOU RIDE 'EM.

After Dwight Eisenhower won the Republican nomination for President from Robert Taft in 1952, a reporter asked Taft about the disappointment that he surely must have felt in setting a goal and not reaching it. Taft admitted, "My great goal was to become President of the United States in 1953." But then he added, "Instead, I became a senator from Ohio!"

Ultimately, Taft's goal was to be elected to a political office and to serve his nation as a representative of the people. And in that he succeeded. If he hadn't run for an office, however, he would never have been elected to one!

That's true for the accomplishment of any real goal in life. You've got to throw your hat into the ring and start pursuing your goal— campaign for its accomplishment the best you know how, thoroughly brief yourself on the

168

issues that are important, define your stance and stay true to it, and maintain a positive attitude even in the face of serious opposition.

You can't cross the finish line if you never leave the starting blocks.

Write the vision, and make it *plain upon tables, that he may run that readeth it.*

HABAKKUK 2:2

A fable is told about a dispute the North Wind had with the Sun about who was the more powerful. They finally agreed to settle their argument with this wager: the first to cause a wayfaring man to strip away his clothing would be the victor.

The North Wind huffed and puffed and blew with all his might, but the more it blew, the closer the traveler wrapped his cloak around him. He finally gave up, and the Sun moved in to have a turn.

The Sun happily shone with all his warmth. As his rays warmed the traveler, he took off first one garment and then the next. At last, nearly overcome by the radiant heat, he undressed completely and plunged himself into a stream for a cool and soothing swim.

> YOU DO NOT LEAD BY HITTING PEOPLE OVER THE HEAD—THAT'S ASSAULT, NOT LEADERSHIP.

The Sun turned to the North Wind and said, "Persuasion is better than force."

Criticism and harsh demands can turn a warm heart cold. Rebellion is more likely to be the result than improved performance. In contrast, praise and encouragement warm the heart. The person who feels appreciated not only follows the leader who gives such applause, but turns in a better performance.

And the servant of the Lord must not strive; but be gentle unto all men, apt to teach, patient.

2 TIMOTHY 2:24

On the night of December 9, 1914, Edison Industries was destroyed by fire. The loss exceeded $2 million, along with the vast majority of Thomas Alva Edison's work. Edison was insured for only $238 because the buildings were constructed of concrete, which at that time, was thought to make a building fireproof. At sixty-seven years of age, Edison watched his life's work go up in flames.

The next morning, after firefighters had finally brought the inferno under control, Edison surveyed his charred dreams and crushed hopes. As he surveyed the scene, he said, "There is great value in disaster. All our mistakes are burned up. Thank God we can start anew."

Three weeks after the fire, Edison Industries produced the first phonograph.

In every setback one can find the seeds of a future success. Such a success, however, will not be automatic. One must plant those seeds with vision, fertilize them with hope and hard work, and continue to water them with enthusiasm.

"For the gate is small, and the way is narrow that leads to life, and few are those who find it."
MATTHEW 7:14 NASB

A Chicago bank once considered a young Bostonian for employment and decided to check out his references, one of whom was an officer at a Boston investment house. The investment executive who responded to the request for a reference wrote that the young man's father was a Cabot, his mother was a Lowell, in his background was a happy blend of Saltonstalls, Peabodys, and other members of Boston's finest families. The man gave his highest recommendation without hesitation!

> DESTINY IS NOT A MATTER OF CHANCE, IT IS A MATTER OF CHOICE. IT IS NOT A THING TO BE WAITED FOR; IT IS A THING TO BE ACHIEVED.

A few days later, the personnel manager of the Chicago bank called the man who had sent the letter and said, "We'd like to have a work reference from you before we hire this young man." The executive replied, "I told you all about him. Didn't you receive my letter?"

The personnel manager replied, "Yes, but we are contemplating using this young man for work, not for breeding purposes."

Your family tree may provide solid roots from which you can grow, but you alone are responsible for the fruit you produce in your life. Genuine purpose in life does not come because others set it up for you; it comes as *you* pursue what *you* desire to achieve and to be.

I press toward the goal for the prize of the upward call of God in Christ Jesus.

PHILIPPIANS 3:14 NKJV

GLDB

IMAGINATION WAS GIVEN TO MAN TO COMPENSATE HIM FOR WHAT HE IS NOT. A SENSE OF HUMOR WAS PROVIDED TO CONSOLE HIM FOR WHAT HE IS.

Ludwig Bemelmans wrote in *My War with the United States* that among the many regulations published by the U.S. Army is a book that gives advice on practical matters to non-commissioned officers. One piece of advice tells an officer how to help soldiers who have quarreled become friends again. The men are to be assigned to wash the same window—one working on the outside, the other inside.

Says Bemelmans, "Looking at each other, they soon have to laugh and all is forgotten. It works; I have tried it."

Laughter shared between friends is one of life's great treasures. Not only is laughter free, but it is a renewable resource, one with countless benefits. It restores a sense of balance to an oppressing day. It builds up energy in a flagging spirit. It helps lighten the load of sorrow, grief, and suffering. It tightens the bonds of relationship.

Laughter has an extremely high rate of return. It brings positive results when we laugh *with* others, rather than laughing *at* them.

A merry heart doeth good like *a medicine.*
PROVERBS 17:22

Bill and Genevieve were at a crossroads. Their baby-sitter had quit, and after several months of shuttling their three young children among friends and grandparents, the strain on the family had grown unbearable. No quality day-care facilities were available in their rural area. They ultimately decided that Gen would continue to work, since the family could live on her salary, and Bill would stay home with the children.

> FAR AND AWAY
> THE BEST PRIZE
> THAT LIFE OFFERS
> IS THE CHANCE
> TO WORK HARD
> AT WORK
> WORTH DOING.

At first, Bill had fun with the children, but then he became frustrated. His self-esteem took a severe hit, and he began to resent his wife's blossoming career. One day while he was cooking dinner, a TV news story caught his attention: two area girls had been abducted and murdered. Bill scooped up his three-year-old and gave her a hug, then went out on the front porch to watch his son walk home from the school bus.

He thought, *If I were at work, I wouldn't be here to watch my children or hug them. I wouldn't have seen our baby daughter take her first steps or see my son get his first hit at Little League . . . I am working. I'm providing for my family—in ways that truly help them to grow.* From then on, when people asked Bill what he did for a living he said, "I'm providing a life for my children."

Wealth obtained by fraud dwindles, but the one who gathers by labor increases it.
PROVERBS 13:11 NASB

GLDB

> DO NOT PERSIST IN FOLLY. IT IS
> NOT A BADGE OF CHARACTER TO
> CONTINUE DOWN THE WRONG ROAD.

For years, "The Wide World of Sports" television program had, as part of its opening sequence, a scene used to depict "the agony of defeat." The scene showed a skier heading down a ski jump in good form, and then for no apparent reason, tumbling head over heels off the side of the jump and bouncing off the supporting structure. The scene caused many viewers to groan in sympathy.

What viewers didn't know, however, was that this particular skier *chose* to fall rather than to finish the jump. He explained later, the jump surface had become slick with ice—much too fast for jumping. Midway down the ramp, he realized that he was picking up so much speed that if he completed the jump, he would very likely land beyond the sloped landing area and hit level ground, which may very well have been fatal. Although it looked messy and painful, by taking the alternative route, the skier actually suffered no more than a headache.

Changing directions in mid-course may sometimes be painful or difficult. Halting a project that seems headed for failure may be challenging and stressful, but that is sometimes the wisest decision to make now in order to succeed later!

The way of a fool is right in his own eyes,
But he who heeds counsel is wise.
PROVERBS 12:15 NKJV

Spain once controlled both sides of the Mediterranean at the Straits of Gibraltar, a powerful position for any seafaring nation. With great pride, the Spanish minted a coin depicting the two Pillars of Hercules—the name given to the promontories of rock on either side of the passageway. Over the pillars, they placed a scroll that said, "ne plus ultra," which means "no more beyond."

> MAN CANNOT DISCOVER NEW OCEANS UNLESS HE HAS THE COURAGE TO LOSE SIGHT OF THE SHORE.

One day, however, bold Spanish sailors made their way through the Straits of Gibraltar and headed for the high seas. They sailed south to Africa, then around its horn to Asia, and eventually across the Atlantic to the New World.

The Spanish wisely rethought their position and stamped a new set of coins. They resembled the old, except that one word had been left off—the word "ne." The new coin read "plus ultra"—"more beyond."

Regardless of your position today, take hope in that there is "more beyond" for you. Life has greater blessings in store for you, and eternity holds the greatest potential for blessings you will ever know.

Now the just shall live by faith: but if any man *draw back, my soul shall have no pleasure in him.*

HEBREWS 10:38

In 1972, *Life* magazine published a story about the amazing adventures of John Goddard. When he was fifteen, John's grandmother said, "If only I had done that when I was young. . . . " Determined not to make that statement at the end of his life, John wrote out 127 goals for his life.

He named ten rivers he wanted to explore and seventeen mountains he wanted to climb. He set goals of becoming an Eagle Scout, a world traveler, and a pilot. Also on his list was: ride a horse in the Rose Bowl parade, dive in a submarine, retrace the travels of Marco Polo, read the Bible from cover to cover, and read the entire *Encyclopedia Britannica.*

He also planned to read the entire works of Shakespeare, Plato, Dickens, Socrates, Aristotle, and several other classic authors. He desired to learn to play the flute and violin, marry, have children (he had five), pursue a career in medicine, and serve as a missionary for his church.

Sound impossible? At the age of forty-seven, John Goddard had accomplished 103 of his 127 goals!

Your list of goals may not be as extensive as John Goddard's, but if you don't have *some* goals in life, you'll find that you have little motivation to get up in the morning, and little satisfaction as your head hits the pillow each night.

Setting goals is not as difficult as it may seem. What do you really want to do? Write it down, then go for it!

But one thing I do: *forgetting what*
lies *behind and reaching forward*
to what lies *ahead.*
PHILIPPIANS 3:13 NASB

A band of juvenile thieves had a well-refined method of operation. They would enter a store as a group. Then, one or two of them would separate from the rest of the group. The others would move to a distant section of the store and start a loud argument, causing enough commotion to grab the attention of the clerks and customers. All eyes would be turned toward the disturbance, leaving the one or two "roving" thieves an opportunity to fill their pockets with merchandise or cash and leave the store before anyone suspected what had happened.

> I THINK THE ONE LESSON I HAVE LEARNED IS THAT THERE IS NO SUBSTITUTE FOR PAYING ATTENTION.

It would be hours, sometimes even days later, before the victimized merchant realized things were missing and call the police. By that time, the thieves were long gone, and there was no possibility of tracing or recovering what had been taken.

Temptation works the same way. It distracts us by using the allure of fame, fortune, power, or satisfaction of fleshly desires. In the process, we are often diverted from critical steps we need to take toward the accomplishment of our goals. When we take our eyes off what is truly important in our lives, we run the risk of losing it!

A wise man will hear and increase in learning, And a man of understanding will acquire wise counsel.

PROVERBS 1:5 NASB

> WHEN WE DO THE BEST THAT WE CAN, WE
> NEVER KNOW WHAT MIRACLE IS WROUGHT
> IN OUR LIFE OR THE LIFE OF ANOTHER.

A Christian man was walking to church one night when he encountered four boys loitering on the street corner. He invited them to go to the service with him. They did, and each of the boys also agreed to return to church with him the next Sunday. They became the nucleus of a Sunday school class the man began to teach.

Years later, a group of the man's friends decided to try to contact the four boys to see what had happened in their lives and to invite them to write a special birthday letter to their teacher to be read at a surprise party. Their letters revealed that one of them had become a missionary to China, one was the president of the Federal Reserve Bank, one was the private secretary to President Herbert Hoover, and the fourth was President Hoover himself!

If you were to hold a handful of pine nuts in your hand today, you could not begin to predict which of the seeds might actually sprout and produce a giant tree. It is amazing that such a large tree might grow from such a small seed. The only way to tell which nuts have trees inside them is to plant them! When you plant acts of kindness and generosity to others you never know what mighty tree may grow from that small seed.

Whatever you do, do it heartily, as to the Lord and not to men.

COLOSSIANS 3:23 NKJV

Dr. Lida Earhart had a reputation for giving her best to any task she undertook. It was that kind of diligence and pursuit of excellence that led to her being the first woman at Columbia University to attain the rank of full professor.

After she retired, she moved to Washington DC and became a parishioner at the New York Avenue Presbyterian Church. One day, a member of the church women's association asked Dr. Earhart to give a talk on the Book of Job during one of the upcoming monthly meetings. She agreed. No doubt the person who extended the invitation was anticipating the basic run-of-the-mill presentation, but she didn't really know Lida Earhart.

> IN LIFE AS IN A FOOTBALL GAME, THE PRINCIPLE TO FOLLOW IS: HIT THE LINE HARD.

Lida studied the Book of Job for two months. She researched the archaeological features of the time of Job and his contemporaries and read numerous commentaries and analyses by biblical scholars. She deeply pondered the book's theme. The result was a presentation that people were still talking about many years later.

What was amazing to her pastor was that she had done all that work for an "ordinary church meeting." Lida, however, didn't know the meaning of *ordinary.*

Leaders are made out of ordinary people who choose to go beyond the ordinary to the extraordinary. That's what sets them apart and makes them leaders.

Whatever your hand finds to do,
do it with all your might.
ECCLESIASTES 9:10 NIV

The famous architect, Sir Christopher Wren, once created a large church dome so unique that his competitors became fiercely jealous. They created such a stir that the authorities responsible for the building insisted that Wren add two supporting pillars to keep the dome from collapsing. Wren explained the integrity of his design and did his best to assure the officials that the dome would not collapse. However, the opposition won out. Wren added the pillars, against his will.

Fifty years later, the dome needed to be repainted. Workers built a scaffold to reach it, and they made an amazing discovery. The two pillars that had been added didn't even touch the ceiling. They were short by two feet! The authorities had only seen the pillars from the ground level, so they assumed they reached the ceiling. The pillars were freestanding and supported nothing. Wren had won his point!

The obstacles and hurdles we put in our own way—and in others' way—are often just as useless as Wren's fake columns. Be sure your objections have merit before demanding that someone answer them!

The sluggard says, "There is a lion in the road! A lion is in the open square!"
PROVERBS 26:13 NASB

When you get what you want in your struggle for self,

And the world makes you king for a day,

Just go to a mirror and look at yourself,

And see what that man has to say.

For it isn't your father or mother or wife,

Whose judgment upon you must pass;

The fellow whose verdict counts most in your life,

Is the one staring back from the glass.

> HE WHO CONQUERS OTHERS IS STRONG. HE WHO CONQUERS HIMSELF IS MIGHTY.

Some people may think you are a straight-shooting chum,

And call you a wonderful guy,

But the man in the glass says you're only a bum,

If you can't look him straight in the eye.

He's the fellow to please, never mind all the rest,

For he's with you clear up to the end,

And you have passed your most dangerous, difficult test,

If the man in the glass is your friend.

You may fool the whole world down your pathway of years,

And get pats on the back as you pass,

But your final reward will be heartache and tears,

If you've cheated the man in the glass.[13]

—Anonymous

He who is slow to anger is better than the mighty, And he who rules his spirit than he who takes a city.

PROVERBS 16:32 NKJV

★ ★

Don't let "Well done" on your
tombstone mean you were cremated!

★ ★

At age five, he wrote an advanced concerto for the harpsichord. Before he was ten, he had published several violin sonatas and was playing the best of Handel and Bach from memory. Soon after his twelfth birthday, he composed and conducted his first opera. He was awarded an honorary appointment as concert-master with the Salzburg Symphony Orchestra and within a few years, was hailed as the pride of Salzburg.

When he died at the age of thirty-five, he had written forty-eight symphonies, forty-seven arias, duets, and quartets with orchestral accompaniment, and more than a dozen operas. He is credited with some 600 original compositions in all!

Even so, Johannes Chrysostomus Wolfgangus Amadeus Theophilus Mozart lived most of his life in poverty and died in obscurity. His sick widow seemed indifferent about his death. A few friends made it to the church for his funeral, but a storm prohibited their going to the graveside for his burial. The location of his grave thus became virtually impossible to identify. No shrine marks his resting place.

What is Mozart's legacy? Not the life he lived, but the music he gave. As with all of us, what we give to the world of our talent and creativity is what lasts.

"His lord said unto him, Well done, thou good and faithful servant: thou hast been faithful over a few things, I will make thee ruler over many things."

MATTHEW 25:21

A surgeon in a large city hospital had a habit of insisting on a few minutes alone before he performed an operation. He had an outstanding reputation as a surgeon, and one of the young doctors who often worked with him wondered if there might be a correlation between this habit and the man's success.

> WHAT COUNTS IS NOT THE NUMBER OF HOURS YOU PUT IN, BUT HOW MUCH YOU PUT IN THE HOURS.

He asked the surgeon about his habit and the surgeon answered, "Yes, there's a relationship. Before each operation, I ask the Great Physician to be with me, to guide my hands in their work. There have been times when I didn't know what to do next in a surgery, and then came the power to go on—power I knew came from God. I would not think of performing an operation without asking His help."

The surgeon's words quickly spread through the hospital, and then across the country. One day a father brought his daughter to the hospital, insisting that the only doctor he would allow to touch her was the one who worked with God.

One of the greatest elements any person can put into his work hours, regardless of the field he is in, is prayer. What motivates you to do your job? What energizes you to do your best? Take some time to cover your work in prayer. You will find that time well spent, as He helps you to achieve more.

Therefore be careful how you walk, not as unwise men, but as wise, making the most of your time, because the days are evil.
EPHESIANS 5:15-16 NASB

> THE WAY FOR A YOUNG MAN TO RISE IS
> TO IMPROVE HIMSELF EVERY WAY HE CAN. . . .

One Friday morning, an eager young student at Stanford University stood before Louis Janin. He was seeking part-time employment from Janin, who informed him, "All I need right now is a stenographer."

"Fine," the young man said eagerly, "I'll take the job." Then he added, "But I can't come back until Tuesday."

Janin agreed and the next Tuesday, the young man reported for work as scheduled. Janin asked him, "Why is it that you couldn't come back before Tuesday?"

The young man replied, "Because I had to rent a typewriter and learn how to use it."

This zealous new typist was Herbert Hoover, whose can-get-it-done attitude eventually led him through the doors of the White House.

No skill you learn will ever be lost to you or prove to be of little use. If nothing more, the learning of new information and new skills builds confidence and exercises the mind. One of the secrets of great leaders is continuing education. Never quit learning! That's what gives you an edge over the competition.

A wise man *will hear, and will increase learning; and a man of understanding shall attain unto wise counsels.*

PROVERBS 1:5

In *McKinney Living,* Robert J. Duncan tells the story of a friend named Cam, who attended the final performance of the Grand Ole Opry at the Ryman Auditorium. When he found himself backstage with an acquaintance, he quickly asked the various stars there to sign the only piece of paper he could find: a one-dollar bill. That dollar bill became Cam's prized possession.

THE ONLY PREPARATION FOR TOMORROW IS THE RIGHT USE OF TODAY.

One morning in the bitter winter of 1976-77, Cam left the station where he worked and noticed a young man sitting in an old yellow Dodge. The car was still there the next day, and the next. Cam asked if something was wrong, and the man told him he had arrived in town for a job that didn't begin for three more days. He had no food and no place to stay. Reluctantly, he asked Cam if he might borrow a dollar. Cam told him he was down to his last dime, but then recalled his Grand Ole Opry dollar. He gave it spontaneously.

The next day, Cam got a job paying $500 for two hours' work. More opportunities began to flow his way. Eventually, Cam was back on his feet financially. He never again saw the man in the old yellow car. Cam only knew that whoever the man was, and whatever principle was in effect, things happened when he gave his "bottom dollar."[14]

*"Take therefore no thought for
the morrow: for the morrow shall
take thought for the things of itself."*
MATTHEW 6:34

A MAN OF HONOR REGRETS A DISCREDITABLE
ACT EVEN WHEN IT HAS WORKED.

Jack Eckerd, founder of the Eckerd Drug chain, which was the second largest drug chain in America at one time, became friends with Chuck Colson a number of years ago. He introduced Colson to various influential groups in Florida in an effort to bring about change in the state's criminal justice system. During their travels together, Chuck had an opportunity to share with Jack about his newfound faith in Jesus Christ. He gave some books to Jack, including his own, and eventually prayed with Jack that he might receive Christ.

Shortly after their prayer, Jack happened to be walking down the magazine aisle in one of his stores, when he noticed *Playboy* and *Penthouse* magazines on the rack, as if for the first time. The presence of the magazines had never bothered him before, but now it did! Jack called the president of his company, and told him, "Take those magazines out of my stores."

"We make three million dollars a year on those magazines," the president argued.

"Take 'em out," Jack insisted. And so it was that these two magazines were removed from 1,700 stores across America in one day.

When Chuck asked Jack about his decision, Jack replied, "Why else would I give away three million dollars? The Lord wouldn't let me off the hook."

A wise man's heart directs him
*toward the right, but the foolish
man's heart* directs him *toward the left.*
ECCLESIASTES 10:2 NASB

Years ago, in Monterey, California, a crisis arose. Monterey had become a paradise for pelicans. After cleaning their fish, the local fishermen would throw the pelicans the entrails. The birds soon became fat and lazy.

Eventually, a new market was found that could use the entrails commercially. The pelicans no longer had a free meal. Yet, the pelicans made no effort to fish for themselves. They just waited, and waited, for the handouts that didn't come. Many starved to death. They seemed to have forgotten how to fish for themselves.

NONE WIL
IMPROVE YO
LOT, IF YOU
YOURSELVE
DO NOT.

The opposite approach was taken by an elderly woman waiting for a bus. She was crippled with rheumatism and loaded down with packages. As the bus door opened, a man offered her a helping hand. The woman smiled and shook her head. "I'd best manage alone," she said. "If I get help today—I'll want it tomorrow."

George Bernard Shaw once noted, "People are always blaming their circumstances for what they are. I don't believe in circumstances. The people who get on in this world are the people who get up and look for the circumstances they want, and if they can't find them, make them."

Study to shew thyself approved unto God.
11 TIMOTHY 2:15

GLDB

WHETHER YOU THINK YOU CAN
OR YOU CAN'T, YOU ARE RIGHT.

Bob Templeton arrived in Barrie, Ontario, shortly after a tornado had struck the town, killing dozens of people and doing millions of dollars worth of damage. Bob, who was vice-president of Telemedia Communications, called a meeting and asked the company's executives, "How would you like to raise three million dollars three days from now in just three hours and give the money to the people of Barrie?" The executives declared, "There is no way we could do that!"

Bob responded by drawing a large "T" on a flip chart. On one side of the T he wrote, "Why we can't" and on the other "How we can." The group began to brainstorm and before long, the "How we can" side had several ideas. The group settled on doing a national radio show featuring well-known broadcasters.

The broadcasters agreed. Stations agreed to broadcast the radiothon. Within three days, fifty stations across Canada participated, and three million dollars was donated by listeners!

Focus on *how* you can get something done that you desire to do, rather than why it might not be possible.

For as he thinketh in his heart, so is he.
PROVERBS 23:7

Napoleon was a genius in sparking patriotism in the common man. He often told this story: Once, while visiting a province he came upon an old soldier in full uniform but with one sleeve hanging empty. He proudly wore the coveted Legion of Honor. Napoleon asked, "Where did you lose your arm?" The soldier answered, "At Austerlitz, sire."

Napoleon asked, "And for that you received the Legion of Honor?" The man said, "Yes, sire. It is but a small token to pay for the decoration." Napoleon continued, "You must be the kind of man who regrets he did not lose both arms for his country."

The one-armed man asked, "What then would have been my reward?" Napoleon answered, "I would have awarded you a *double*

THE RECIPE FO
PERPETUAL
IGNORANCE IS
BE SATISFIED WI
YOUR OPINION
AND CONTEN
WITH YOUR
KNOWLEDGE

Legion of Honor." And with that, the proud old fighter drew his sword and immediately cut off his other arm.

Napoleon told the story for years before someone asked him, "How?"

A similar story is told of the man who collected thousands of dollars for the grieving mother of the "unknown soldier."

It's not wrong to question what you *think* you know. Sometimes it's wrong *not* to.

Do you see a man wise in his own eyes?
There is more hope for a fool than for him.
PROVERBS 26:12 NASB

GLDB

> BEGIN TO ACT BOLDLY. THE MOMENT
> ONE DEFINITELY COMMITS ONESELF,
> HEAVEN MOVES IN HIS BEHALF.

Early in the twentieth century, Sir Ernest Shackleford made a voyage to Antarctica. He had a dream of crossing the 2,100 miles of the icy continent by dog sled. Shackleford's ship, however, ran into an ice pack nearly two hundred miles from land, and sank.

He and his men trudged across drifting ice floes to reach land, and then continued on to the nearest outpost, nearly 1,200 miles away. They pulled the only supplies they were able to salvage from their sinking ship in a lifeboat— a ton of weight—behind them as they made their way on foot.

When they reached waters clear enough to navigate, they faced waves as high as ninety feet! They finally reached South Georgia Island and were told later that the expanse of water they crossed had never been crossed before.

Seven months after they set sail, the group finally reached their destination, the chosen point for *beginning* their trek across Antarctica. They were so bedraggled that their friends didn't even recognize them.

When asked about the experience, each man said that he had felt the presence of One unseen, who had guided them. Each man had a sense that he was not alone and that he *would* survive.

You're never alone; you'll make it! Take a bold step of faith, and watch what God will do.

Let us therefore come boldly unto the throne of grace, that we may obtain mercy, and find grace to help in time of need.
HEBREWS 4:16

When Chris Gross of Santa Clara, California, heard about the 137 children who lost at least one parent in the bombing of a federal building in Oklahoma City, he thought, *Where would I be if my folks weren't around when I was growing up?* With that motivation, he set up a college fund for those children.

His first step was to call the CEO of his company and tell them he was going to set up a fund, and that he would be donating his annual salary as an investment analyst—all $53,874 of it—to the fund. He then challenged his company and eighteen others to match his gift, so that the fund might reach one million dollars. "It's not easy living without a paycheck," Gross has admitted, but the 26-year-old has no debts and lives frugally with four roommates.

> WASTE NO MORE TIME ARGUING WHAT A GOOD MAN SHOULD BE. BE ONE.

Word of Gross's sacrificial gift quickly spread through the Central Coast region of California, and many residents responded with personal gifts. Several benefit shows, concerts, and seminars were held, including benefits by the San Francisco Opera and the San Francisco Giants.

Can one man's example make a difference? Within four months, the fund Gross established had $525,000 in it!

... be an example (pattern) for the believers in speech, in conduct, in love, in faith, and in purity.

1 TIMOTHY 4:12 AMP

TAKE CALCULATED RISKS. THAT IS QUITE DIFFERENT FROM BEING RASH.

Dr. Evan O'Neill Kane, chief surgeon of the Kane Summit Hospital in New York, had been fascinated for years by the possibility of using local anesthetics in areas where general anesthetics had traditionally been used. He was especially eager to discover if an appendectomy could be performed with only a local.

After performing nearly 4,000 such operations in his four decades as a surgeon, Dr. Kane was confident that the operation was suitable for local anesthesia, but it was tough to find someone willing to stay awake through such a surgery.

Then, on February 15, 1921, he found such a patient. He prepped the patient, then deftly removed the troublesome appendix. The patient felt no pain and recovered nicely. The operation was considered an overwhelming success.

The patient was none other than Dr. Kane himself. He had succeeded in removing his own appendix under local anesthetic, thus paving the way for many patients to have similar operations, without the complications and difficulties sometimes experienced with general anesthesia. A risky move, certainly, but not an uncalculated one.

The risk you take today may give many a bright tomorrow!

The plans of the diligent lead *surely to advantage, But everyone who is hasty* comes *surely to poverty.*
PROVERBS 21:5 NASB

Many children are taught that the magic words are "Please" and "Thank you." As good as these are, Sir William Osler once offered a different opinion:

"Though a little one, the master word looms large in meaning. It is the 'Open Sesame' to every portal, the great equalizer in the world, the true philosopher's stone which transmutes all the base metal of humanity into gold. The stupid man among you it will make bright, the bright man brilliant, and the brilliant student steady.

THERE IS NO SUBSTITUTE FOR HARD WORK.

"With the magic word in your heart, all things are possible, and without it all study is vanity and vexation. The miracles of life are with it; the blind see by touch, the deaf hear with eyes, the dumb speak with fingers.

"To the young it brings hope, to the middle-aged confidence, to the aged repose. The true balm for hurt minds, in its presence the heart of the sorrowful is lightened and consoled. Not only has it been the touchstone of progress, but it is the measure of success in everyday life . . . the master word is *work*."

Today, choose to work gratefully, not grudgingly. Work is a necessity for maintaining anything of lasting value.

Do you see a man skilled in
his work? He will serve before kings;
he will not serve before obscure men.
PROVERBS 22:29 NIV

219

TALK LOW, TALK SLOW, AND DON'T SAY TOO MUCH.

A young computer salesman named Kurt was delighted when one of his clients expressed interest in buying a used computer system—one that Kurt had installed two years ago, but had recently been replaced by an upgrade. After careful calculation and consultation with his home office, he fixed a price of $800,000 for the used system and documented all his reasons for requesting that amount.

As he sat down to negotiate, he heard an inner voice say, "Wait. Let them do the initial talking." The buyers quickly filled the silence with a long rundown of their own research about this particular computer system's strengths and weaknesses, the age of the equipment, and the need for new software. "Can you throw upgraded software into the deal?" one of the buyers asked. "Sure," Kurt offered. The buyers then said, "We'll give you $950,000 for the system, but not a penny more."

Less than an hour later, the paperwork was signed and Kurt walked away with a better deal than he had imagined, having said little more than, "Thank you."

Sometimes the best thing to say is, *nothing!*

Do not be hasty in word or impulsive in thought to bring up a matter in the presence of God.
ECCLESIASTES 5:2 NASB

Former President Ronald Reagan enjoyed telling the following story about himself. He claimed it was how he learned, early in life, to make firm and resolute decisions.

According to the story, a kindly aunt once took him to a cobbler to have a pair of shoes custom-made for him. The shoemaker asked, "Do you want a square toe or a round one?" The young Reagan hemmed and hawed, so the cobbler said, "Come back in a day or two and tell me what you want."

INDECISION IS OFTEN WORSE THAN THE WRONG ACTION.

A few days later the cobbler saw Reagan on the street and asked what he had decided about the shoes. "I haven't made up my mind," Reagan answered.

"Very well," the cobbler said, and then he announced to his customer, "Your shoes will

222

be ready tomorrow." When Reagan got the shoes, one had a round toe and the other a square toe!

Reagan concluded, "Looking at those shoes every day taught me a lesson. If you don't make your own decisions, somebody else will make them for you."

Remember always that no decision is a decision!

A double minded man is
unstable in all his ways.

JAMES 1:8

IT IS BETTER TO TAKE A RISK NOW THAN ALWAYS TO LIVE IN FEAR.

One simply cannot live without taking risks. Risk is woven into every aspect of our daily experience!

To laugh is to risk appearing the fool.

To weep is to risk appearing sentimental.

To reach out for another is to risk involvement.

To expose feelings is to risk exposing our true self.

To place your ideas, your dreams, before the crowd is to risk loss.

To love is to risk not being loved in return.

To live is to risk dying.

To hope is to risk despair.

To try at all is to risk failure.

(Author Unknown)

Even so, the greatest hazard in life is to risk nothing. Because the person who risks nothing

- accomplishes nothing,

- has nothing,

- feels nothing,

- and in the end, becomes nothing.

Don't be afraid to take a calculated risk. Risk is essential for growth in every area of life.

The Lord is my helper, and I will not fear what man shall do unto me.

HEBREWS 13:6

In *The Finishing Touch*, Chuck Swindoll tells about a man he met one Thanksgiving: "With a grin and a twinkle, he whipped out his hand. It was a hand you could strike a match on, toughened by decades of rugged toil. 'You look like a man who enjoys life. What do you do for a living?' I asked.

'Me? Well, I'm a farmer from back in the Midwest.'

"'Really?'...[He] then told me about his plans for traveling on his own through California. 'What did you do last week?' I asked. His answer stunned me. 'Last week I finished harvesting 90,000 bushels of corn,' he said with a smile.

"I then blurted out, 'Ninety thousand! How old are you, my friend?' He didn't seem at all hesitant or embarrassed by my question. 'I'm

CARPE DIEM— SEIZE THE DAY!

just a couple months shy o' ninety.' He laughed again as I shook my head.

"He had lived through four wars, the Great Depression, sixteen presidents, ninety Midwest winters, who knows how many personal hardships, and he was still taking life by the throat. I had to ask him the secret of his long and productive life. 'Hard work and integrity' was his quick reply. As we parted company, he looked back over his shoulder and added, 'Don't take it easy, young feller. Stay at it!'"[15]

"The kingdom of heaven suffereth violence, and the violent take it by force."

MATTHEW 11:12

GENIUS IS DIVINE PERSEVERANCE.

Comedienne Joan Rivers was devastated by the suicide of her husband and manager, Edgar Rosenberg. She tells about working through her grief in her book *Still Talking*. One of the things Rivers discovered during her experience was a deep inner strength. She says, "What will I be doing in five years? I'm not worried—whether I am single, or married to a wonderful man.

"I'd love to be doing television, but nothing is secure in show business. Even if things go badly, the bottom I might hit would be nowhere near as deep as what I have been through. I have become my version of an optimist. If I can't get through one door, I'll go through another—or I'll *make* a door. Something terrific will come no matter how dark the present.

"God always comes up with a third-act twist. . . . That's the exhilaration of being alive. There is always another scene coming out of nowhere. God is the best dramatist."

It is often difficult for a person to realize when they are going through a crisis that they are doing just that—going *through* it. All crises are temporary! All storms eventually pass. Every night turns into a new morning. Choose to persist until you see the breaking of dawn!

Having done all, to stand. Stand therefore.
EPHESIANS 6:13-14

Henry Ford was once asked, "How can I become a success?" Ford replied, "If you start something, finish it!"

Ford learned this lesson early in his career. When he began work on his first automobile, he worked many long but exciting hours in a little brick building behind his home. Such enthusiasm overtook him that he found it hard to take time out to eat or sleep. Before he had completed his first car, however, he became acutely aware that he could build an even better car.

NO PLAN IS WORTH THE PAPER IT IS PRINTED ON UNLESS IT STARTS YOU DOING SOMETHING.

He was so sure of the need for improvements that the thrill and enthusiasm for his first car began to lessen. *Why spend all that time finishing a car that he already knew was inferior?* Still, something inside him forced him to continue, to focus his total energy on the first car and finish what he had started, before he allowed himself to fantasize about a second car.

As it turned out, Ford said he learned even more about how to improve the second car by finishing every detail of his original car. If he had given in to the temptation to quit building the first car, he may never have made any car at all.

Many people strive to be perfectionists, but the *completionists* usually accomplish more in life.

Write the vision And make it plain on tablets, That he may run who reads it.
HABAKKUK 2:2 NKJV

231

> *"I CAN'T DO IT" NEVER YET
> ACCOMPLISHED ANYTHING;
> "I WILL TRY" HAS PERFORMED WONDERS.*

A father once looked in on his 16-year-old son as he sat at the desk in his bedroom, struggling to finish his algebra homework. The father quickly scrawled a note and tacked it on the bulletin board above his son's desk. It said DETERMINATION. "What's that?" his son asked.

"You're dealing with all these formulas," the dad explained. "X plus Y and all that. So I made up my own formula to encourage you. It's try plus determination!"

In her autobiography titled **Dolly,** Dolly Parton says, "My high school was small. So during a graduation event, each of us got a chance to stand up and announce our plans for the future. 'I'm going to junior college,' one boy would say. 'I'm getting married and moving to Maryville,' a girl would follow. When my turn came, I said, 'I'm going to

Nashville to become a star.' The entire place erupted in laughter. I was stunned. Somehow, though, that laughter instilled in me an even greater determination to realize my dream. I might have crumbled under the weight of the hardships that were to come had it not been for the response of the crowd that day. Sometimes it's funny the way we find inspiration."[15]

Give your dream a try today, no matter what others say.

I can do everything through
him who gives me strength.

PHILIPPIANS 4:13 NIV

Peter Cartwright was a nineteenth-century circuit-riding Methodist preacher. He had a reputation for being a hard preacher and an uncompromising man.

One Sunday morning as he was about to take the pulpit, he was told that President Andrew Jackson was in the congregation. He was warned not to say anything out of line, anything that might be controversial to the President.

Cartwright stood to preach and immediately announced, "I understand that Andrew Jackson is here. I have been requested to be guarded in my remarks. Andrew Jackson will go to hell if he doesn't repent."

The congregation was shocked. They sat in stunned silence, wondering how the President might respond. Jackson didn't flinch.

After the service, President Jackson sought out Peter Cartwright to shake his hand. He said, "Sir, if I had a regiment of men like you, I could whip the world."

It is never a compromise to tell the truth. Your audience may change, but the truth remains the same.

Righteous lips are *the delight of kings; and they love him that speaketh right.*

PROVERBS 16:13

GLDB

NO MATTER WHAT YOU DO, DO
YOUR BEST AT IT. IF YOU'RE GOING TO
BE A BUM, BE THE BEST BUM THERE IS.

Abraham Lincoln once made these two statements, as he evaluated the decisions he was making in his attempts to heal a war-torn nation:

"I desire so to conduct the affairs of this administration that if at the end, when I come to lay down the reins of power, I have lost every other friend on earth, I shall at least have one friend left, and that friend shall be down inside of me.

"I do the very best I know how; the very best I can; and I mean to keep on doing it to the end. If the end brings me out all right, what is said against me will not amount to anything. If the end brings me out all wrong, then a legion of angels swearing I was right will make no difference."

Whatever you are doing, and in whatever conversation you find yourself engaged give it

- your whole heart,

- your undistracted attention,

- and your maximum energy.

Give your all to each task you choose to do; give your best creativity to each idea you ponder. You may not be the greatest success in the world, but you will have made a success of your world.

Whatsoever ye do, do it heartily, as to the Lord, and not unto men.

COLOSSIANS 3:23

A story is told of Freddie Follow-the-Leader. Freddie went to the college of his friends' choice. He pursued a history major solely because his girlfriend had also chosen that major. He took a job with a certain company because his friend thought it was a good firm.

Freddie moved into a large new home because a colleague had just purchased one. He bought a new car because the neighbors had one. Before long, Freddie found himself in deep water financially, and he was sinking fast!

> THE GRASS MAY LOOK GREENER ON THE OTHER SIDE, BUT IT STILL HAS TO BE MOWED.

One of his friends told him about a new multilevel sales company and told him that he was making a killing. So Freddie signed on. He had never sold anything, and he wasn't all that sure about the product or the scheme, but he thought, *All my friends are doing it.* He borrowed the money to get started.

Several months later when the company folded, Freddie not only lost the money he had invested, but also his job. He had been devoting too much time and energy to his new enterprise. This in turn, caused him to lose his new house and fancy car.

And the friends Freddie had been following? They were nowhere in sight!

God created each of us with unique gifts, and He has a unique plan for each of our lives. Pursue only what you know is right for you. That's the road to success—*your* road.

Be content with such things as ye have.
HEBREWS 13:5

> ★
>
> IDENTIFY YOUR HIGHEST SKILL AND
> DEVOTE YOUR TIME TO PERFORMING IT.
>
> ★

When William Carey first began considering the possibility of going to India as a pioneer missionary, his father pointed out to him that he possessed no academic qualifications that would fit him for such a task. Carey answered, "I can plod."

Plodding may not be a *skill,* but if you can truly find the one thing you are good at doing, which you enjoy doing, and then plod steadily forward in development of that skill, you have a great possibility for achievement.

When Carey went to India, this was his typical day: he arose at 5:45 A.M. to read a chapter of the Hebrew Bible and have private devotions. At 7 A.M. he led family prayers in Bengali, read Persian with a tutor and a portion of Scripture in Hindustani. After breakfast, he translated Sanskrit into English. At 10 A.M. he went to college to teach until 2 P.M., then translated into Bengali until dinnertime. After an early supper, he translated into Sanskrit and studied the Telugu language until he preached to an English congregation at 7:30 P.M. About 9 P.M. he returned to translating for two hours, wrote to a friend in England, read a chapter from his Greek Testament, and then finally went to bed.

Such plodding yielded great results for the Gospel!

Wherefore the rather, brethren, give diligence to make your calling and election sure: for if ye do these things, ye shall never fall.
2 PETER 1:10

Murray Spangler, a department store janitor in Canton, Ohio, decided the only way to overcome the boredom of his job—which basically consisted of sweeping the floors—was to find a more innovative way to do it! His job also made him wheeze and cough, which was added incentive to seek out a better method.

Why not eliminate the broom? he thought. And then a second thought came, *Maybe there's another way to get the dust up. Maybe even suck up the dust.*

EVEN A WOODPECKER OWES HIS SUCCESS TO THE FACT THAT HE USES HIS HEAD.

Spangler's questions led him to invent a crude, but workable vacuum cleaner. He then sought out an old friend in the leather business to finance the manufacturing of his invention. The man's name was H. W. Hoover . . . not only did Hoover Vacuum Cleaners become very popular, but "hoovering" became, for at least one generation, synonymous with sweeping floors!

You may be working with the latest technology today, but even so, there is always a **better** way to perform the basic tasks of your job. Think creatively about your work. Question the methods and equipment you are using. The next great invention might just be one idea away!

The wise have eyes in their head,
but fools walk in darkness.
ECCLESIASTES 2:14 NRSV

> MILLIONS SAW THE APPLE FALL, BUT
> NEWTON WAS THE ONE WHO ASKED WHY.

When nine-year-old Shantee began having trouble with her homework, Mary Pinkney decided to set an example for her grand-daughter and an older cousin, Alvin. She told a writer for *Woman's Day:*

"Shantee needed help with third-grade math, and I couldn't do it. I knew then that I needed to go back to school—not just so I could help myself, but also to give my grandchildren the help they needed."

Pinkney had dropped out of grade school to get married, more than forty years before and was now sixty-one years old. Even so, she returned to school, attending at night while holding down a full-time day job at a seafood plant. It took her four years to complete her studies for a high school diploma, but she made the grade!

Shantee became an honor roll student in the process. As for Alvin, he was inspired to complete his own high-school degree and go to college. He said, "She showed me I could do it too." Mary was so inspired by Alvin that she joined him to study computer technology at Brunswick College![16]

There's more to an education than knowledge. There's also the *inspiration* factor—sometimes being an inspiration to others, and sometimes inspiring yourself!

Get wisdom: and with all thy getting
get understanding.

PROVERBS 4:7

In his book *Lyrics,* Oscar Hammerstein I[I] speaks on the issue of excellence: "A year or so ago, on the cover of the New York *Herala Tribune* Sunday magazine, I saw a picture of the Statue of Liberty . . . taken from a helicopter, and it showed the top of the statue's head. I was amazed to see the detail there. The sculptor had done a painstaking job with the lady's coiffure, and yet he must have been pretty sure that the only eyes that would see this detail would be the uncritical eyes of seagulls.

"He could not have dreamt that any man would ever fly over this head. He was artist enough, however, to finish off this part of the statue with as much care as he had devoted to her face and her arms and the torch and everything that people can see as they sail up the bay. . . .

EVERY JOB IS A S
PORTRAIT OF T
PERSON WHO D
IT. AUTOGRAP
YOUR WORK
WITH EXCELLEN

"When you are creating a work of art, or any other kind of work, finish the job off perfectly. You never know when a helicopter, or some other instrument not at the moment invented, may come along and find you out."

Excellence for the Christian is not merely a matter of rising to the best of human standards. It is a matter of doing things "as unto the Lord" and for His pleasure, honor, and glory.

Many ... have done well,
but you excel them all.
PROVERBS 31:29 NKJV

> THERE IS MORE CREDIT AND SATISFACTION
> IN BEING A FIRST-RATE TRUCK DRIVER
> THAN A TENTH-RATE EXECUTIVE.

President Woodrow Wilson once had a maid who continually lamented the fact that she and her husband needed more prestigious positions in life. She approached the President one day after the Secretary of Labor had resigned from the cabinet.

"President Wilson," she said, "my husband is perfect for this vacant position. He is a laboring man, knows what labor is, and understands laboring people. Please consider him when you appoint the new Secretary of Labor."

Wilson replied, "I appreciate your recommendation, but you must remember, the Secretary of Labor is an important position. It requires an influential person."

"But," the maid countered, "if you made my husband the Secretary of Labor, he would be an influential person!"

No title can make you something that you are not, in talent, skill, and ability. A reputation is developed from the inside out! You will make your job important, far more than any job will ever make you important.

The sluggard craves and gets nothing, but the desires of the diligent are fully satisfied.

PROVERBS 13:4 NIV

A ***Washington Post Magazine*** article by Richard Cohen tells the story of Albie, an elderly handyman: "Albie touches things the way sculptors do, with the authority of a man who works with his hands. Lumber is his marble. His fingers roam the surface— searching out what, I'm not sure. . . . Albie built a little trash-can shed for the neighbors up the road. It had three compartments, one for each can . . . each lid worked perfectly, the hinges precisely positioned.

"Albie painted the shed green and let it dry. I went to look at it, amazed that a man had made it, that it had not been bought somewhere. I put my finger to the smooth paint. Done, I thought. But the next day Albie came back with a machine and roughed up the paint. Every so often he would probe with his fingers. He was adding another coat. . . .

> THE MAN WHO IS BORN WITH A TALENT WHICH HE WAS MEANT TO USE FINDS HIS GREATEST HAPPINESS IN USING IT.

"At the end of the day when Albie gathers his tools, places them in the truck and drives off, he leaves behind a swirl of dust and at least one person who wonders why Albie gets paid so little for doing so much. But then again, his is quiet, individual work. There are no meetings or memos. He is alone with his thoughts. And he is master of all he surveys. A fine definition, I think, of freedom."[17]

But life is worth nothing unless
I use it for doing the work
assigned me by the Lord Jesus.
ACTS 20:24 TLB

*********** Circulus Æquinoctialis *********** 〷 ***********************

FOR ALL YOUR DAYS PREPARE, AND MEET
THEM EVER ALIKE; WHEN YOU ARE THE ANVIL,
BEAR—WHEN YOU ARE THE HAMMER, STRIKE.

****

A blacksmith works at his forge, using his well-muscled arm to strike hearty blows on the hot bars of iron before him. His project is a great chain, the kind used to hold the anchor of a ship. The blacksmith does his work faithfully and well. Every link is made of good metal, and all are soundly welded together. Months, then years, go by. The old blacksmith dies and is forgotten.

A ship sets out to sea and on its voyage, is engulfed by a raging storm. The captain orders that the anchor be cast. Fierce winds and high waves threaten the vessel. The entire crew, and most of the passengers, know their fate depends on whether the chain will hold their ship to the anchor. All through the dark night and raging storm the anchor holds fast and at last, the storm abates. All aboard greet the dawn with gladness and a hymn of thanksgiving to God for their deliverance.

Does the story have a hero? Of course. The one who wielded a simple hammer and anvil with skill and good conscience—steadily doing his work and riding out the waves of his own life to create the best he could for others.

How many such heroes are there, unsung, yet true? You can be one, too.

Study to shew thyself approved unto God, a workman that needeth not to be ashamed.
2 Timothy 2:15

Not every young bull makes it into a bullfighting arena. Bulls are carefully selected to play their part in this sport.

One of the last tests for a young bull occurs within a bullfighting arena, far from the eyes and shouts of a crowd. A bull is jeered on only by a target holding a waving cape—a target that is actually a picador riding a padded horse. With each charge, the picador pricks the young bull with a lance. The bull's bravery is carefully rated according to how many times the bull is willing to continue to charge its target, in spite of the sting of the pic. Cowardly bulls are sent to the slaughterhouse.

> A MAN IS NOT FINISHED WHEN HE IS DEFEATED. HE IS FINISHED WHEN HE QUITS.

Human beings may not literally be put to the "picador test," but the same principle holds true for us nonetheless. Those who give up when they feel the sting of a rebuff, a rejection, an insult, or a rebuke are those who will never realize their full potential for achievement. It is those who endure the stinging words and actions of others and who press on, again and again taking a running charge at their goals, who will score accomplishments.

Let us not be weary in well doing: for in due season we shall reap, if we faint not.

GALATIANS 6:9

GLDB

The late James Herriott, author of numerous best-selling books about his veterinary practice in England, has a counterpart in Bean Blossom, Brown County. His name is Dr. James Brester. A quiet, shy man, he is often misunderstood by his human clients who can't always understand his mumbling. His animal patients, however, always seem to respond to his gentle touch.

The man is a legend to those who live in rural Brown County. He has a reputation for never giving up on a case, even those an animal's owner might consider hopeless. He takes on all types of patients. He has even been known to ride a runaway llama down a hill while administering its shot.

There are also thousands of quieter tales of the vet's compassion and kindness. He has an amazing list of patients—32,000 and still counting. Yet he lives almost as simply as he did when he was a student. Doc Brester says that he simply loves his work, but hates to charge for it.

Doc Brester is a servant—not only to beast, but to men and women who love their pets, need their work animals, and rely on healthy stock for their livelihood. His greatest achievement? His reputation!

"To be the greatest, be a servant."
MATTHEW 23:11 TLB

Thomas Edison was the guest of the governor of North Carolina one day. As they talked together, the governor complimented Edison on his inventive genius.

"I am not a great inventor," Edison said.

"But you have over a thousand patents to your credit, haven't you?" the governor asked.

"Yes, but about the only invention I can really claim as absolutely original is the phonograph," said Edison.

"I'm afraid I don't understand what you mean," countered the governor.

> GENIUS IS ONE PERCENT INSPIRATION AND NINETY-NINE PERCENT PERSPIRATION.

"Well," explained Edison, "I guess I'm an awfully good sponge. I absorb ideas from every course I can and put them to practical use. Then I improve them until they become of some value. The ideas which I use are mostly the ideas of other people who don't develop them themselves."

You do not necessarily need to do something original in your life in order to succeed. You only need to do something *well.*

For just as the body without the *spirit is dead, so also faith without works is dead.*
JAMES 2:26 NASB

GLDB

WE MAKE A LIVING BY WHAT WE GET—
WE MAKE A LIFE BY WHAT WE GIVE.

Andrew Carnegie is considered by most historians to be one of the richest and most ruthless of the "robber barons" who flourished at the beginning of the twentieth century. His lasting legacy, however, is as a man who gave.

Some 2,505 libraries bear his name, and they are only a small part of his philanthropic effort.

In his later years, Carnegie once demanded of his accountants, "How much have I given away so far?"

The accountants knew down to the last dollar: "$324,657,399 to be exact." Carnegie blinked and gulped when he heard the figure. And then he recovered from his own astonishment to exclaim, "Good heavens, where did I get all that money?"

Statues are not sculpted in honor of misers.

Monuments are not erected in memory of those who have a reputation for stinginess.

Names of honor are not given to those who hoard.

One of the best ways to make it into the annals of history, as well as into the goodwill of others, is to be a person noted for generosity.

"It is more blessed to give than to receive."
ACTS 20:35 NASB

Bill Campbell, owner of Campbell's Restaurant Equipment & Supply in San Luis Obispo, California, was surprised to find a $10 bill in his mail one day. It was from a customer who had purchased a refrigerator from his company in 1963.

The note attached to the bill said: "I was under-charged $10. When the salesman called to inform me, I refused to pay the $10. I have suffered with this all these years. So here's the $10. Thanks."

Campbell, whose father started the business in 1939, only vaguely remembers hearing about an irate customer who was undercharged and refused to pay. The details are fuzzy in his memory. He said about the incident, "That was $10 we wrote off." He can't help but wonder, however, if the man may have received more than his

> HONESTY IS
> THE CORNERSTONE
> OF ALL SUCCESS,
> WITHOUT WHICH
> CONFIDENCE AND
> ABILITY TO
> PERFORM SHALL
> CEASE TO EXIST.

money's worth out of the refrigerator. In fact, he suspects the refrigerator is still running.

To Campbell, the $10 is too valuable to put in the bank. It's more important to him as a conversation piece, framed and hanging on his wall. Campbell wishes, however, that the customer would have given his name or a return address. "He needs a word of thanks," says Campbell. "He did fess up to it."

Let me be weighed on honest scales,
That God may know my integrity.
JOB 31:6 NKJV

GLDB

> IF A TASK IS ONCE BEGUN, NEVER LEAVE IT
> TILL IT'S DONE. BE THE LABOR GREAT OR
> SMALL, DO IT WELL OR NOT AT ALL.

Robert stuttered badly as a young boy growing up in Brooklyn. On days he knew he would be called upon in class, he played hooky. At age fifteen, he quit school to deliver shoes and dresses for his father and uncle in Manhattan.

One day his mother, who had a beautiful voice, heard him singing around the house and took him to a voice instructor whose studio was in the Metropolitan Opera House. Robert was awe struck. The man agreed to teach Robert on a scholarship, and Robert began to sing in earnest. Between deliveries, he sang. At night he sang and went to lessons.

Not long after, while making a delivery on Fifty-seventh Street, he saw a crowd at Steinway Hall and learned that auditions were being held for a summer job at Scaroon Manor, an Adirondack resort. He got the job, beating out more than forty competitors. Only eighteen with no real stage experience, he was determined to succeed. He did it all that summer—singing show tunes and backup for chorus girls, being the straight man for a young comedian named Red Skelton.

Baritone Robert Merrill went on to give 800 performances at the Metropolitan Opera House. He has sung for nine Presidents, and he is still singing, *still* developing his talent.

Whatever your hand finds to do,
do it with your might.
ECCLESIASTES 9:10 NKJV

Most people think of John Wesley as a powerful preacher, and indeed, he was. What many people do not know, however, is how prolific he was. He averaged 3 sermons a day for fifty-four years, preaching a total of more than 44,000 times in his life. In doing this, he traveled by horseback and carriage more than 200,000 miles—about 5,000 miles a year. For even a very productive man, that would seem to be a full-time effort.

Still, John Wesley found time to write and edit. His published works include a four-volume commentary on the entire Bible, a five-volume work on natural philosophy, a four-volume work on church history, and a dictionary of the English language. He also wrote histories of England and Rome, grammars on the Hebrew, Latin, Greek,

OUR DAYS ARE IDENTICAL SUITCASES—ALL THE SAME SIZE—BUT SOME PEOPLE PACK MORE INTO THEM THAN OTHERS.

French, and English languages, three works on medicine, six volumes of church music, seven volumes of sermons and controversial papers, and he edited a library of fifty volumes known as "The Christian Library."

He habitually rose at 4 A.M. and retired at 10 P.M., allowing only brief periods for meals. Yet he declared, "I have more hours of private retirement than any man in England."

Making the most of your time.
EPHESIANS 5:16 NASB

GLDB

Graffiti has become a major problem in many American cities, a problem some officials have declared impossible to resolve. Jane Golden believes otherwise. For years, Golden worked as a major mural artist in California and had thousands of fans.

Then, ill with lupus and weary of seeing her work vandalized by graffiti, she moved back to her roots in the East. She settled in Philadelphia and launched a program to deal with the wall-scrawlers who had destroyed her work. She sought to make them fall in love with murals!

Golden became associated with Tim Spencer, who founded Philadelphia's Anti-Graffiti Network, a neighborhood program that involves kids in painting city murals. The youth attend workshops in the fall and winter, then paint in the spring and summer. More than 30,000 youngsters participated in the program in its first seven years, painting some 900 murals—virtually none of them have ever been defaced with graffiti.

Rather than bemoan the defacing of plain walls, perhaps more cities should turn plain walls into works of art. Seeing the potential for good in something is nearly always the first step in turning an impossibility into a *possibility.* After all, that's how God sees each one of us!

> *"With men this is impossible; but with God all things are possible."*
>
> MATTHEW 19:26

On a foggy morning in July 1952, Florence Chadwick waded into the chilly waters off of Catalina Island. Her goal? To swim the channel to the California coast.

The water was numbing cold that day. The fog was so thick she could barely see the boats that were accompanying her. Several times, a rifle was fired to scare away sharks that approached her.

She swam more than fifteen hours before she asked to be taken out of the water. Her trainer tried to encourage her to swim on since they were so close to land.

> IN LIFE, AS IN FOOTBALL, YOU WON'T GO FAR UNLESS YOU KNOW WHERE THE GOAL POSTS ARE.

Florence was not a stranger to long-distance swimming. She was the first woman to swim the English Channel in both directions. But that day, she was discouraged. When she looked ahead all she saw was fog. Florence gave up only one-half mile from her goal!

Later, she said, "I'm not excusing myself, but if I could have seen the land, I might have made it." It wasn't the cold water, exhaustion, or fear that caused Florence to fail that day. It was the fog. Two months later, Florence Chadwick swam the Catalina channel and set a new speed record.

Keep your goals in sight today and press on. You may be much closer to fulfilling them than you realize!

Where there *is no vision, the people perish.*
PROVERBS 29:18

GLDB

IN THE RACE TO BE BETTER OR BEST,
DON'T FORGET TO ENJOY THE JOURNEY!

Commentator Earl Nightingale, whose name is virtually synonymous with radio broadcasting excellence, once said: "We read about people who sail around the world in a thirty-foot sailboat or overcome handicaps to win a gold medal at the Olympics, and we later find they're stories about persistence.

"I remember well the day I sat down to write the first of my radio programs. That was more than twenty years ago, more than fifty-two hundred programs ago, the equivalent of thirty-six full-length books. Certainly no world's record, but a good example of what persistence can do.

"When we see the tired faces of commuters on the big city subway, and children climbing aboard the school bus, we see persistence at work. We see it in the expression of a housewife doing grocery shopping or the week's laundry. But everything we do contributes to the life we lead, the joys we experience, the satisfactions we realize from time to time. And persistence itself is a joy when we're doing what we enjoy and want to do. Not a very complicated formula, is it?"

Be happy … and rejoice and be glad-hearted continually (always).
1 THESSALONIANS 5:16 AMP

In *The Finishing Touch,* Chuck Swindoll tells of a time when a friend stopped by his study to "speak the truth in love" to him. The man said, "I don't think you'll fall morally or ethically. What does worry me is that you could be tempted to let your time with God and your time in the study of the Scriptures become less and less important to you. I want to urge you: *Do not let that happen.*"

IT'S ONE OF THE HARDEST THINGS IN THE WORLD TO ACCEPT CRITICISM ... AND TURN IT TO YOUR ADVANTAGE.

Swindoll took his words to heart and wrote down these five promises to himself:

- *I promise* to keep doing original and hard work in my study. Those to whom I am called deserve my best efforts.

- *I promise* to maintain a heart for God. That means I will pray frequently and fervently and stay devoted to Him and to my calling.

- *I promise* to remain accountable. Living the life of a religious Lone Ranger is not only unbiblical, it's dangerous.

- *I promise* to stay faithful to my family. My wife deserves my time, affection, and undivided attention. Our now-grown children deserve the same.

- *I promise* to be who I am. Just me. I plan to keep laughing, saying things a little "off the wall," being a friend, and making a few mistakes each month.[18]

Now no chastening seems to be joyful for the present, but painful; nevertheless, afterward it yields the peaceable fruit of righteousness to those who have been trained by it.

HEBREWS 12:11 NKJV

N

> HERE IS A PIECE OF ADVICE THAT IS WORTH
> A KING'S CROWN: TO HOLD YOUR HEAD UP,
> HOLD YOUR OVERHEAD DOWN.

Early in his career as a master salesman, Victor Kiam worked for Playtex, selling girdles and bras in Mississippi. One day, when he arrived at a small shop, he found the owner sweeping the floor. Kiam introduced himself, extended his hand, and paused. He was met with silence. Undaunted, he opened his sample case and began to make his pitch.

Suddenly, the store owner flew into a rage, and he began sweeping Kiam out of his store. Within moments, Kiam found himself flat on his back, dust swirling around him.

Rather than fight back, Kiam was determined to find out why this man was so upset with him. He talked with other sales reps and eventually got to the root of the problem. His predecessor had done *too* good a job, causing this man to become so overstocked with merchandise that too much of the man's capital was tied up in inventory. Kiam immediately arranged for one of his larger accounts to purchase the man's excess inventory at cost. Kiam not only received a very warm greeting the next time he showed up with his sample case, but he made a friend.

One of the best ways to build any relationship is to help another person solve a problem.

Any enterprise is built by wise planning, becomes strong through common sense, and profits wonderfully by keeping abreast of the facts.

PROVERBS 24:3-4 TLB

The sculptures of Michelangelo need no introduction to most people. We are all familiar with his masterpieces, *David, Day and Night, Madonna of Bruges, Twilight and Dawn, La Pieta, Medici Madonna and Child.*

One of his most massive sculptures is a statue of Moses, completed more than four hundred years ago, often called his best work.

If one looks closely at the statue of Moses, however, you will find a long, narrow dent on Moses' knee. It is the mark of an artist who was never satisfied with his own work!

> SUCCESS SEEMS TO BE CONNECTED WITH ACTION. SUCCESSFUL PEOPLE KEEP MOVING. THEY MAKE MISTAKES, BUT THEY DON'T QUIT.

After completing the statue, Michelangelo is said to have cried, "Why dost thou not speak?" He fully expected to make cold marble come to life! In anger at what he perceived to be a failure, Michelangelo struck the knee of the statue with his chisel.

Those who are satisfied with their accomplishments tend to remain as little as the things they do. The true giants in any field are those who are never satisfied that they have done enough or have done their best. That's the driving force behind their greatness.

Let us throw off everything that
hinders ... and let us run with
perseverance the race marked out for us.
HEBREWS 12:1 NIV

GIVE ME A STOCK CLERK <u>WITH</u> A GOAL, AND I WILL GIVE YOU A MAN WHO WILL MAKE HISTORY. GIVE ME A MAN <u>WITHOUT</u> A GOAL AND I WILL GIVE YOU A STOCK CLERK.

During the days when the United States was taking shape as a nation, Andrew Bradford had an enviable business contract. His company was given the responsibility of doing all the public printing for the new state of Pennsylvania.

Bradford's company had a reputation for sometimes producing shoddy work, and unfortunately, that was the verdict when Bradford was asked to print an important address the governor was planning to deliver. The document was put together in a careless, unimpressive manner.

Another young printer saw this example of sloppy work as a great opportunity. He prepared an elegant document of the speech, and forwarded it with his compliments to the governor and each member of the assembly. He was soon awarded the contract for all of Pennsylvania's public printing. His name? Benjamin Franklin.

Franklin replaced what was inferior with something that was of quality and excellence. That's the mark of a successful product, no matter what it is—even our own emerging life.

Fixing our eyes on Jesus ... who for the joy set before Him endured the cross ... and has sat down at the right hand of the throne of God.
HEBREWS 12:2 NASB

Luther Burbank was a man who loved nature deeply, and it seemed Mother Nature loved him in return. In the course of his career he created many new plants—hybrids that made plants more beneficial or beautiful. He puttered around in his garden for fifty years unlocking botanical secrets.

He made potatoes that grow larger, whiter, and more delicious than ever before. He developed a spineless desert cactus that cattle could fatten upon, and he also caused the blackberry to shed its thorns. He grew plums without pits and strawberries that would ripen year round.

GREAT MINDS HAVE PURPOSE; OTHERS HAVE WISHES.

Trees became more frost resistant, and walnut shells became thinner. Daisies grew more beautiful, calla lilies became more aromatic, and the dahlia was given a new fragrance. The amaryllis gained color, and numerous new flowers were added to the world's greenhouse.

Burbank had a kind and gentle manner, approaching every plant as if it were a child—with its own face, promise, and unique character. He saw himself as a man who only encouraged a plant to fulfill God's plan and potential for its life.

He knew his own purpose and sought to fulfill it. He knew each plant has a purpose and sought to fulfill it. God has a plan for your life—a purpose. Just as Burbank coaxed new things out of established plants, God leads you and guides you and coaxes you into each new level of growth, always at the right season.

"For I know the plans I have for you,"
declares the LORD, "plans to prosper you …
to give you hope and a future."
JEREMIAH 29:11 NIV

The story is told of a salesman whose company—a large concern that manufactured electric fans and air conditioning units—sent him to Central Africa. Within days he called his boss, saying, "Please bring me home. This is a total waste of company time and effort. Nobody uses fans and air conditioners here." The company brought him home. Six months later, they sent another salesman to the region.

This time, the salesman began to call in order after order. His supervisor asked, "How is that you are selling so many units where our previous man couldn't make a single sale?" The man replied, "I don't know. It's so hot here. *Everybody* could use a little cool air!"

Opportunity is nearly always related to one's perspective on a situation. The founders of the Southern Baptist Convention were honored with a plaque that was placed at the

First Baptist Church of Augusta, Georgia where the Convention was first organized in 1845. The plaque recognizes this approach to opportunity in describing the founding fathers as "Men who see the invisible, hear the inaudible, believe the incredible, and think the unthinkable!" What a prelude to opportunity!

A man's gift maketh room for him, and bringeth him before great men.
PROVERBS 18:16

A window-washing company was washing the exterior windows of a condominium complex one day. One of the crew members mistakenly began to wash the windows of a unit that was not on the schedule. The owner of the condominium came rushing out and said to the window washer, "I didn't order this service. I have no intention of paying you for this work."

The man washing the windows thought fast on his feet and replied, "That's okay. Every time we do a condominium complex, we do one extra unit 'on the house' to show owners such as yourself what a fine job we do, and to show you what you are missing."

The owner of the unit was so impressed that he signed on for the service the next time the company visited his complex. The company

> MAKE EVERY DECISION AS IF YOU OWNED THE WHOLE COMPANY.

executives, hearing of his tact, decided to adopt this approach as a sales gimmick. It turned out to be the best boost to business the company had ever experienced, and the quick-thinking employee earned a raise.

Give some thought to what you would do to improve your company if you were suddenly made the CEO or owner. Then find a way to implement your ideas, or share them with someone who *can!*

*He that handleth a matter wisely
shall find good.*
PROVERBS 16:20

> HE WHO CONSIDERS HIS WORK BENEATH
> HIM WILL BE ABOVE DOING IT WELL.

"Sophie the scrub woman" daily scrubbed the steps of a large New York City building. One day a man stopped and said to her, "Sophie, I understand that you are a child of God."

"Yes, sir," Sophie replied, "I'm a child of the King!"

"Well, as a child of the King, do you believe that God recognizes you as a princess?"

Sophie beamed. "He certainly does!"

"Well, if God your Father is your King, and you are a princess, don't you think it is beneath you to be found here in New York City scrubbing these dirty steps every day?"

Sophie continued to work as she said, "There's no humiliation whatever. I'm not scrubbing these steps for my boss. I'm scrubbing them for Jesus Christ, my Savior!

What He did for me was far greater than anything I can ever do for Him."

As the man walked away, he heard Sophie say:

I cannot work my soul to save
For that my Lord has done;
But I can work like any slave
For love of God's dear Son.

(Author Unknown)

"The greatest among you will be your servant."
MATTHEW 23:11 NRSV

William James, psychologist and author, believed in "moral muscles." He encouraged his patients to do at least one good deed every day, just to stay "morally fit." He believed that a person becomes strong psychologically by resisting life's small temptations and by doing deeds that an average person might otherwise find tedious, inconsequential, or even distasteful. To James, staying strong on the inside was related more to what one does than to what one thinks or says.

> SUCCESS IS THE RESULT OF WORKING HARD, PLAYING HARD, AND KEEPING YOUR MOUTH SHUT.

James' approach is a little like that of the mythological farm boy—a weakling who was ridiculed by all the other lads in the area. One day the youth rescued a newborn calf by picking it up and carrying it to the barn. The next day, the boy went out and held the calf in his arms, to comfort and befriend it.

The boy continued that practice day after day. Since the calf's weight increased only a little each day, the youth didn't notice that he was lifting ever-greater weight. As the calf grew larger, he got stronger. Eventually, the farm boy was lifting a full-sized bull and was hailed as the strongest lad in five counties.

There's a great deal to be said for daily plodding. You travel further in life by quietly moving forward, than by just talking about your destination.

Even a fool is thought to be wise when he is silent. It pays him to keep his mouth shut.
PROVERBS 17:28 TLB

In *Living, Loving and Learning,* Leo Buscaglia says: "I always talk about Julia Child. I really like her attitude. *She's* someone I would write to. I watch her because she does such wonderful things: 'Tonight we're going to make a soufflé.' And she beats this and she whisks that, and she throws things on the floor. She wipes her face in her napkin and she does all these wonderful human things. Then she takes this soufflé and throws it in the oven, and talks to you a while. Then says, 'Now there's one ready.' When she opens it up, it caves in. You know what she does? She doesn't kill herself. She doesn't commit hara-kiri with her butcher knife. She says, 'Well, you can't win 'em all. Bon appetit!' I love it! That's the way we have to lead our lives. You can't win 'em all. . . .

"But I know people who are still flagellating themselves over mistakes that they made twenty years ago. 'I should have done this,' and 'I should have done that.' Well, it's tough that you didn't. But who knows what surprises there are in tomorrow? Learn to say 'Bon appetit.' . . . Nobody said you were perfect. It might even be more interesting. You burned the dinner, so you go out."[19]

Though he fall, he shall not be utterly cast down: for the LORD upholdeth him with his hand.

PSALM 37:24

In *The Hiding Place,* Corrie Ten Boom tells of tense times her family experienced in Holland during the German invasion. One night, as Corrie tossed restlessly on her bed while war bombers droned overhead and artillery burst nearby, she heard her sister downstairs in the kitchen.

Unable to sleep, she arose and joined Betsie for a cup of tea. The two talked well into the night, until the sound of the bombers died away. They knew that explosions had ripped an area nearby, but all had become quiet.

> I WOULD RATHER WALK WITH GOD IN THE DARK THAN GO ALONE IN THE LIGHT.

As Corrie stumbled through the darkness back to her room, she reached down to pat her pillow before laying down. As she did, something sharp cut her hand. It turned out to be a ten-inch-long piece of jagged metal! She cried out for her sister and raced back down the stairs holding the shrapnel in her hand.

As Betsie bandaged her hand, she said repeatedly, "On your pillow!"

Corrie said, "Betsie, if I hadn't heard you in the kitchen. . . . "

To this her sister firmly said, "Don't say it, Corrie! There are no 'ifs' in God's world. The center of His will is our safety."

Corrie later took that message around the world: "God's will is our hiding place."

Even when walking through the dark valley of death I will not be afraid, for you are close beside me, guarding, guiding all the way.

PSALM 23:4 TLB

★★★★★★★★★★★★★★★★★ ✦ ★★★★★★★★★★★★★★★★★

YOU MUST HAVE LONG-RANGE GOALS
TO KEEP YOU FROM BEING FRUSTRATED
BY SHORT-RANGE FAILURES.
★★★★★★★★★★★★★★★★★★★★★★★★★★★★★★★★★★★

A man once approached a construction site and noticed three men shoveling dirt out of a long ditch. He asked the first man what he was doing. The man sneered back with a surely-you-can-figure-it-out-yourself attitude, "Digging a ditch."

He walked on to the next man and asked the same question. The reply was only slightly more kind, "I'm makin' a living. Just makin' a living. Gotta feed the wife and kids, you know."

When he asked the third man what he was doing, the man said with a great deal of positive energy and pride, "Sir, I am creating part of a masterful set of irrigation channels that are going to turn this dry ol' valley into a garden rich with produce to feed the world's hungry!"

Look beyond the seemingly meaningless chores and minor failures of today and see a bigger picture—ultimately, one that serves others. You'll find greater satisfaction in your daily grind if you see yourself as making jewels for the Lord's crown, rather than simply polishing rocks.

For the vision is yet for an appointed time.... Though it tarries, wait for it; Because it will surely come.

HABAKKUK 2:3 NKJV

The story is told of a man who was starting a computer sales and service company. He advertised for qualified sales people and began interviewing those who applied. One day, into his office walked a man who had obviously come from a very rural area. He was wearing jeans and a plaid shirt but had managed to find a tie somewhere in his closet.

"Mister," he said after heartily shaking the owner's hand, "I'd shore like a chance to work in your 'bidness.'" The owner explained that he was looking for someone with experience in computers—the man had only a personal home computer—but to each argument the owner put forward, the young man replied, "I think I could learn that. I'd shore like a chance."

> IT TAKES MORE TO PLOW A FIELD THAN MERELY TURNING IT OVER IN YOUR MIND.

The owner decided he'd give the young man a month to prove himself. After several days of training, he sent the man out to sell.

One day he saw a note on the man's desk. It had three lines scribbled on it: "Gotta call fifteen people today. Gotta sell two systems this week. Gotta make $1,000 a month." After six months, the man hadn't come close to his goals. He had actually sold nine systems in only fourteen days, and he earned more than $75,000 in commissions in his first six months!

Faith by itself, if it is not accompanied by action, is dead.

JAMES 2:17 NIV

> TRUE CONTENTMENT IS THE POWER
> OF GETTING OUT OF ANY SITUATION
> ALL THAT THERE IS IN IT.

Joni Eareckson-Tada has written in *Decision* magazine, "A large part of me never moves, because I'm paralyzed from the shoulders down. It's like instant stillness! I don't run, I sit. I don't race, I wait. . . . "

"My 'natural' stillness used to drive me crazy. After my diving injury, I lay still for three months waiting to be moved from the intensive care unit into a regular hospital room. . . . While in rehab, I stayed put in my wheelchair for hours outside physical therapy . . . and in the evenings my stillness would madden me as I sat by the door waiting for friends or family to come for a visit. It was more frightening at night when I lay down . . . at least in my wheelchair I could flail my arms and shrug my shoulders, but in bed I couldn't move at all except to turn my head on the pillow. My bed was an altar of affliction.

"But time, prayer and study in God's Word have a way of changing things. Now, many years later, my bed is an altar of praise. It's the one spot where I always meet God in total, relaxed stillness. In fact, as soon as I wheel into my bedroom and see the side lamp lit, it signals in my mind: 'It's time to be still and to know more about God . . . it's time to pray.'"[20]

I have learned the secret of being content in any and every situation.
PHILIPPIANS 4:12 NIV

When the father of the famous philosopher Emmanuel Kant was an old man, he made a dangerous journey by foot through the forests of Poland to his native country of Silesia. On the way, he was accosted by a band of robbers who demanded all his valuables. Kant's father turned over all that he had as the robbers repeatedly demanded, "Have you given us everything?" Each time, the old man replied, "All." They allowed him to proceed, threatening to kill him if he revealed their deed.

> PEOPLE MAY DOUBT WHAT YOU SAY, BUT THEY WILL BELIEVE WHAT YOU DO.

After hurriedly walking several hundred yards down the road, the man felt something hard strike his shin. He suddenly remembered that he had sewn a gold piece into the hem of his robe several years ago. At once he hurried back to the robbers and said to them, "I told you what was not true; it was unintentional. I was too terrified to think. Here, take the gold in my robe." To the man's astonishment, none of the robbers made a move to cut open the hem of his garment. Rather, one went to his saddlebag and handed him back his purse of money. Another restored to him his book of prayer, and still another helped him back on his horse. In the end, the robbers asked him for a blessing before he rode away.

Inside, people can recognize God's good-ness when they see it. It moves people and inspires them. It changes lives.

My little children, let us not love in word,
neither in tongue; but in deed and in truth.
1 JOHN 3:18

GLDB

★ ★ ★ ★ ★ ★ ★ ★ ★ ★ ★ ★ ★ ★ ★ ✦ ★ ★ ★ ★ ★ ★ ★ ★ ★ ★ ★ ★ ★ ★ ★

THE RIGHT ANGLE TO APPROACH A
DIFFICULT PROBLEM IS THE "TRY-ANGLE."

★ ★

In 1989, Rainier School, Washington's largest state facility for mentally retarded adults, faced a serious problem. Tens of thousands of mosquitoes, flies, and other insects invaded the 500-acre facility. Inspectors cited the insects as a health hazard.

Anita Glasco, a counselor at the school, recalled that the previous year, inspectors had cited the school as having a sanitation problem, owing to the great number of birds that had peppered the sidewalks with their droppings. Numerous bird nests had been removed. She also recalled hearing at her garden club that swallows eat large numbers of insects. Glasco approached Rainier's administrators and suggested that the residents in the school's vocational-education program build birdhouses and place them at the perimeter of the acreage to attract swallows. The chairman agreed to give the idea a try!

After only a few weeks, the birdhouses had been installed, swallows had taken up residence, and the insect problem began to disappear. The extra birdhouses the residents made were sold to pay for materials and to reward the workers.

The *worst* thing you can do with a good idea is to polish it up and set it on a shelf. Always give your ideas a try!

I can do all things through
Christ who strengthens me.
PHILIPPIANS 4:13 NKJV

A family once moved into a new apartment and soon found themselves besieged by salesmen desiring to sign them up for everything from laundry service to life insurance. One day, a dairyman came to the door offering his services. The woman of the house said, "No, my husband and I don't drink milk."

"Be glad to deliver a quart every morning for cooking," the dairyman persisted. "That's more than I need," she replied, trying to close the door.

"Well, ma'am, how about some cream? Berries comin' in now, and. . . . " She answered curtly, "No, we never use cream."

The dairyman walked away slowly and the woman congratulated herself on her sales resistance. The following morning, however,

THE DIFFERENCE BETWEEN ORDINARY AND EXTRAORDINARY IS THAT LITTLE EXTRA.

she answered a knock at the door only to find this same dairyman at the door, a bowl of ripe strawberries held carefully in one hand and a half pint of cream in the other.

"Lady," he said, as he poured the cream over the berries and handed them to her, "I got to thinkin'. If you've never used cream on berries, you sure have missed a lot in life." Needless to say, he delivered to her house every day thereafter!

When met with resistance, a leader will use creativity and kindness to overcome obstacles. Don't take "no" for an answer; just approach the issue from a different angle. God is a creative God. He can give you that little "extra" every day!

In a race, everyone runs but only one person gets first prize. So run your race to win.

1 Corinthians 9:24 TLB

ALL OUR DREAMS CAN COME TRUE—IF
WE HAVE THE COURAGE TO PURSUE THEM.

Glenn Cunningham was born on a Kansas farm and educated in a one-room schoolhouse. He and his brother were responsible for keeping the school's fire going. One morning as the boys poured kerosene on the live coals to get the fire started before school, the stove blew sky high.

Glenn rushed toward the door, but then realized his brother had fallen and wasn't moving. He rushed back to help, suffering terrible burns in the process. In the end, his brother died, and Glenn was hospitalized with severe burns on his legs.

The tragedy seemed to mark an end to Glenn's dream of running track. Still, he was determined to walk again—which the doctors had said wouldn't happen—but he did! Then, he began to run. Through many periods of

308

discouragement and disappointment, Glenn kept running, ever faster.

He mastered the mile. Eventually, he set his sights on the international record for his distance, and he broke it! He finally held the world record of his dreams.

What kept Glenn running? He dedicated his races to the memory of his brother, as he was determined to transform the greatest tragedy of his life into a blessing. He may have had scarred legs, but he had a *whole* heart.

Be strong and courageous, and act;
do not fear nor be dismayed, for the
LORD God, my God, is with you.

1 CHRONICLES 28:20 NASB

REFERENCES

Unless otherwise indicated, all Scripture quotations are taken from the *King James Version* of the Bible.

Scripture quotations marked NIV are taken from the *Holy Bible, New International Version*®. NIV®. Copyright © 1973, 1978, 1984 by International Bible Society. Used by permission of Zondervan Publishing House. All rights reserved.

Scripture quotations marked AMP are taken from *The Amplified Bible, Old Testament* copyright © 1965, 1987 by Zondervan Corporation, Grand Rapids, Michigan. *New Testament* copyright © 1958, 1987 by The Lockman Foundation, La Habra, California. Used by permission.

Verses marked TLB are taken from *The Living Bible,* copyright © 1971. Used by permission of Tyndale House Publishers, Inc., Wheaton, Illinois 60189. All rights reserved.

Scripture quotations marked NASB are taken from the *New American Standard Bible.* Copyright © The Lockman Foundation 1960, 1962, 1963, 1968, 1971, 1972, 1973, 1975, 1977, 1995. Used by permission.

Scripture quotations marked NRSV are taken from the *New Revised Standard Version* of the Bible, copyright © 1989 by the Division of Christian Education of the National Council of the Churches of Christ in the USA. Used by permission. All rights reserved.

Scripture quotations marked NKJV are taken from *The New King James Version* of the Bible. Copyright © 1979, 1980, 1982, 1994 by Thomas Nelson, Inc., Publishers. Used by permission.

ACKNOWLEDGMENTS

We acknowledge and thank the following people for the quotes used in this book: John D. Rockefeller, Jr. (8), Dr. Eugene Swearingen (10), Winston Churchill (12,124), Katherine Graham (14), Arnold Bennett (16), Peter J. Daniels (18), Samuel Johnson (20,146,192), Benjamin Franklin (22,158), Lillian Dickson (24), Cervantes (26,42), Michelangelo (28), Don Herold (30), Zig Ziglar (32,92), Jean Sibelius (34), Harvey MacKay (36), Sebasstien-Roche (38), Ralph Waldo Emerson (40,150), Johann Wolfgang von Goethe (44,204,242), Henry David Thoreau (46), Dennis Waitley (48,248), Friedrich Wilhelm Nietzsche (50,68), James Huxley (52), Diane Ravitch (54), Roger von Oech (56), Dwight D. Eisenhower (58,162), Mark Twain (60,74), St. Francis de Sales (62,142), E.M. Kelly (64), Henry Ford (38,200), Aeschylus (72), Gorden van Sauter (76), Margaret Fuller (78), William James (80), Edward Gibson (82), Solon Bale (84), Elbert Hubbard (88,202), Bessie Stanley (90), David J. Schwartz (96), St. Francis Xavier (98), John A. Shedd (100), Lucius Annaeus Seneca (102), George Herbert Palmer (104), William Feather (106), Isaac Singer (108), a Jesuit motto (110), Lawrence D. Bell (112), George Herbert (114), Bill Cosby (116), J.R.R.Tolkien (120), Robert Frost (124), Marcel Pagnol (126), Charles Dickens (130), Euripides (134), Martin Luther King, Jr. (136), Milton S. Gould (138), William Carey (144), Robert Browning (146), Catherine Booth (148), Jim Rohn (152), Edward Young (154), Sam Snead (156), David Mahoney

(158), Mary Webb (160), G.K. Chesterton (164,292), William Jennings Bryan (166), Horace Walphole (168), Theodore Roosevelt (170,182), Baltasar Gracian (172), Ronald E. Osborn (176), Diane Sawyer (178), Helen Keller (180), Lao-Tze (186), Michael Aspen (188), Abraham Lincoln (192), H. L. Menken (196), Bertolt Brecht (198), Marcus Aurelius (206), George S. Patton (208), Thomas Alva Edison (210,250), John Wayne (212), Gerald R. Ford (214), Thomas Fuller (216), Horace (218), Woodrow Wilson (220), William Danforth (222), George P. Burnham (224), James L. Hayes (226), Robert Mitchum (228), Ronald Brown (232), Barbara Baruch (236), B.C. Forbes (240), Edwin Markham (244), Richard Nixon (246), Mary Kay Ash (254), Louis D. Brandels (260), Arnold Glasow (262), J. C. Penney (266,272), Ruth Boorstin (268), Conrad Hilton (270), Washington Irving (274), Francis Bacon (276), Robert Townsend (278), Alexander Chase (280), Albert Einstein (282), Edward John Phelps (284), Mary Gardiner Brainard (286), Charles C. Noble (288), Walt Disney (300).

ENDNOTES

[1] Catherine Marshall, *A Closer Walk* (Ada, MI: Fleming H. Revell Co., 1986) pp. 102-103.

[2] *Good Housekeeping* (July 1995).

[3] Lloyd John Ogilvie, *Let God Love You* (Dallas: Word, 1974) pp. 139-140.

[4] Edith Schaeffer, *What Is a Family?* (Ada, MI: Fleming H. Revell Company, 1975) p. 149.

[5] *Working Woman* (May 1995).

[6] Steven Carter and Julia Sokol, *Lives Without Balance* (New York: Villard Books, Random House, Inc., 1991) pp. 125,194.

[7] James Hewett, *Illustrations Unlimited* (Wheaton: Tyndale, 1988) p. 142.

[8] *Reader's Digest* (June 1995).

[9] Catherine Marshall, *A Closer Walk* (Ada, MI: Fleming H. Revell, 1986) p. 27.

[10] *Encyclopedia of 7700 Illustrations,* Paul Lee Tan (ed.), (Rockville, MD: Assurance Publishers, 1979) p. 216.

[11] Stan Mooneyham, *Traveling Hopefully* (Dallas: Word, 1984) pp. 90-91.

[12] *Fortune* (May 1, 1995).

[13] *Speaker's Sourcebook,* Glenn Van Ekeren (ed.), (Englewood Cliffs, NJ: Prentice Hall, 1988) p. 187.

[14] Robert J. Duncan, *McKinney Living* (McKinney, TX: self-published, 1982) p. 82.

[15] *Reader's Digest* (March 1995).

[16] *Woman's Day,* July 18, 1995, p. 80.

[17] *Washington Post Magazine* (July 29, 1990).

[18] Charles R. Swindoll, *The Finishing Touch* (Dallas, TX: Word, 1994) pp. 144-145.

[19] Leo Buscaglia, *Living, Loving and Learning* Steven Short (ed.), (New York: Holt, Rinehart & Winston, 1982) p. 260.

[20] *Decision* (September 1994).

Additional copies of this book and other titles
in the *God's Little Devotional Book* series
are available from your local bookstore.

Also look for our
Special Gift Editions in this series.

God's Little Devotional Book
God's Little Devotional Book for Couples
God's Little Devotional Book for Dads
God's Little Devotional Book for Graduates
God's Little Devotional Book for Men
God's Little Devotional Book for Moms
God's Little Devotional Book on Prayer
God's Little Devotional Book for Students
God's Little Devotional Book on Success
God's Little Devotional Book for Women

Honor Books
Tulsa, Oklahoma

If you have enjoyed this book,
or if it has impacted your life,
we would like to hear from you.
Please contact us at:

Honor Books
Department E
P.O. Box 55388
Tulsa, Oklahoma 74155

or by e-mail: info@honorbooks.com